W9-CNL-606

student book volume **2**

Cultural, Social and Technical

MATHEMATICS

Secondary Cycle Two, Year Three

Claude Boivin
Dominique Boivin
Antoine Ledoux
Étienne Meyer
François Pomerleau
Vincent Roy

LES ÉDITIONS
CEC
A Quebecor Media Company

9001, boul. Louis-H.-La Fontaine, Anjou (Québec) Canada H1J 2C5
Telephone: 514 351-6010 • Fax: 514 351-3534

ORIGINAL VERSION

Publishing Manager
Véronique Lacroix

Production Manager
Danielle Latendresse

Coordination Manager
Rodolphe Courcy

Project Manager
Dany Cloutier
Diane Karneyeff

Proofreader
Viviane Deraspe

Graphic Design
Dessine-moi un mouton

Technical Illustrations
Stéphan Vallières

General Illustrations
Rémy Guenin

Geographical Maps
Les Studios Artifisme

Iconographic Research
Esther Ste-Croix

The authors and publisher wish to thank the following people for their collaboration in the evolution of this project.

Expert Collaborator
Richard Cadieux, teacher, École secondaire
Jean-Baptiste-Meilleur, CS des Affluents

Scientific Consultant
Matthieu Dufour, professor, UQAM

Pedagogical Consultants
Josée Bédard, teacher, École secondaire
Les Etchemins, CS des Navigateurs

Geneviève Morneau, teacher, École secondaire
Mgr-Richard, CS Marguerite-Bourgeoys

Stéphane Rompré, teacher, École secondaire
Léopold-Gravel, CS des Affluents

Mélanie Tremblay, professor, UQAR

ENGLISH VERSION

Translation of *Visions*, Culture, société et technique, manuel de l'élève, volume 2, 3e année du 2e cycle du secondaire by i-Edit inc.

These programs are funded by Quebec's Ministère de l'Éducation, du Loisir et du Sport, through contributions from the Canada-Québec Agreement on Minority-Language Education and Second-Language Instruction.

Les Éditions CEC Inc. thank the Government of Québec for the financial assistance granted for the publishing of this book through the Tax credit for book publishing program, administered by SODEC.

Visions, Cultural, Social and Technical, Student Book,
Volume 2, Secondary Cycle Two, Year Three
© 2010, Les Éditions CEC inc.
9001, boul. Louis-H.-La Fontaine
Anjou (Québec) H1J 2C5

Translation of *Visions*, Culture, société et technique, manuel de l'élève, volume 2, 3e année du 2e cycle du secondaire
ISBN 978-2-7617-2800-3
© 2010, Les Éditions CEC inc.

Legal Deposit: 2010
Bibliothèque et Archives nationales du Québec
Library and Archives Canada

ISBN 978-2-7617-2803-4

Printed in Canada
1   2   3   4   5   14   13   12   11   10

TABLE OF CONTENTS

volume 2

Graphs 2

    Graphs

REVISION 4

    • Tree diagrams and networks
    • Polygon
    • Solid

SECTION 3.1
The characteristics of a graph 12

    • Graph
    • Connected graph
    • Complete graph

SECTION 3.2
Paths and circuits 22

    • Simple path and simple circuit
    • Euler path and Euler circuit
    • Hamiltonian path and Hamiltonian circuit

SECTION 3.3
Weighted graphs and
directed graphs 33

    • Tree
    • Directed graph
    • Weighted graph

SECTION 3.4
Optimization using graphs 45

    • Path of minimum value
    • Tree of minimum or maximum values
    • Chromatic number
    • Critical path

CHRONICLE OF THE PAST
Claude Berge 60

IN THE WORKPLACE
Performance-venue
technical directors 62

OVERVIEW 64

BANK OF PROBLEMS 74

**Probability and
voting procedures** 78

   Probability

REVISION 80

- Random experiment
- Event
- Probability of an event
- Random experiment with several steps
- Weighted mean

SECTION 4.1
Types of events 88

- Logical connectors
- Venn diagrams
- Mutually exclusive events and non-mutually exclusive events
- Independent events and dependent events

SECTION 4.2
Conditional probability 98

- Conditional probability

SECTION 4.3
Voting procedures 107

- Majority rule
- Plurality rule
- Borda count
- Condorcet method
- Elimination vote
- Approval voting
- Proportional representation

SECTION 4.4
Decision-making in the
context of social choices 118

- Majority rule and plurality voting
- Borda count, Condorcet method, elimination method and approval voting
- Majority election
- Proportional representation

CHRONICLE OF THE PAST
Nicolas de Condorcet 128

IN THE WORKPLACE
Politicians 130

OVERVIEW 132

BANK OF PROBLEMS 140

REFERENCE . . 145
Technology 146
Knowledge 152

PRESENTATION OF STUDENT BOOK

This *Student Book* contains two chapters each called "Vision." Each "Vision" presents various learning and evaluation situations (LES), a "Revision" section and special features "Chronicle of the past," "In the workplace," "Overview" and "Bank of problems." At the end of the *Student Book*, there is a "Reference" section.

REVISION

The "Revision" section helps to reactivate prior knowledge and strategies that will be useful in each "Vision" chapter. This feature contains several activities designed to review prior learning, a "Knowledge summary" which provides a summary of the theoretical elements being reviewed and a "Knowledge in action" section consisting of reinforcement exercises on the concepts involved.

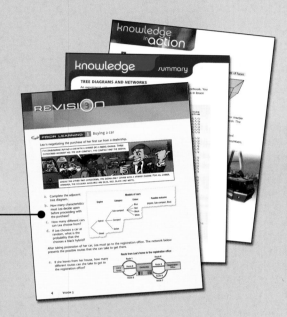

THE SECTIONS

A "Vision" chapter is divided into sections, each starting with a problem and a few activities, followed by the "Technomath," "Knowledge" and "Practice" features. Each section is related to a LES that contributes to the development of subject-specific and cross-curricular competencies, as well as to the integration of mathematical concepts that underscore the development of these competencies.

Problems

The first page of a section presents a problem that serves as a launching point and is made up of a single question. Solving the problem engages several competencies and various strategies while calling upon the mobilization of prior knowledge.

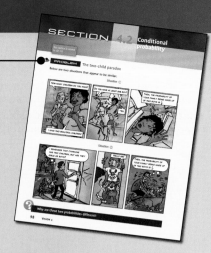

Activity

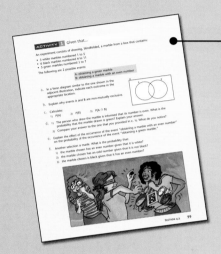

The activities contribute to the development of subject-specific and cross-curricular competencies, require the use of various strategies, mobilize knowledge and further the understanding of mathematical notions. These activities can take on several forms: questionnaires, material manipulation, construction, games, stories, simulations, historical texts, etc.

Technomath

The "Technomath" section allows students to use technological tools such as a graphing calculator, dynamic geometry software or a spreadsheet program. In addition, the section shows how to use these tools and offers several questions in direct relation to the mathematical concepts associated with the content of the chapter.

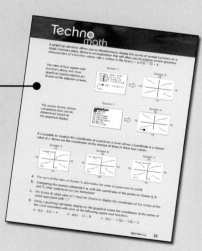

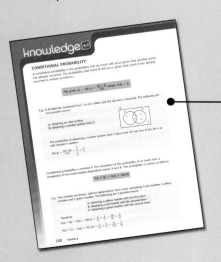

Knowledge

The "Knowledge" section presents a summary of the theoretical elements encountered in the section. Theoretical statements are supported with examples in order to foster students' understanding of the various concepts.

Practice

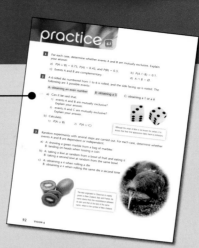

The "Practice" section presents a series of contextualized exercises and problems that foster the development of the competencies and the consolidation of what has been learned throughout the section.

Chronicle of the past

The "Chronicle of the past" feature recalls the history of mathematics and the lives of certain mathematicians who have contributed to the development of mathematical concepts that are directly related to the content of the "Vision" chapter being studied. This feature includes a series of questions that deepen students' understanding of the subject.

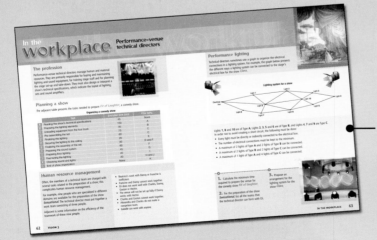

In the workplace

The "In the workplace" feature presents a profession or a trade that makes use of the mathematical notions studied in the related "Vision" chapter. This feature includes a series of questions designed to deepen students' understanding of the subject.

Overview

The "Overview" feature presents a series of exercises and problems that integrate and consolidate the competencies that have been developed and the mathematical notions studied.

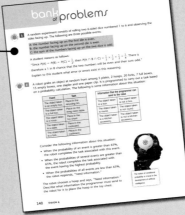

The "Knowledge in action," "Practice," "Overview" and "Bank of problems" features include the following:
- A number in a blue square refers to a Priority **1** and a number in an orange square a Priority **2**.
- When a problem refers to actual facts, a keyword written in red uppercase indicates the subject with which it is associated.

Bank of problems

This feature ends each "Vision" and presents problems, most of which are in context, each of which focuses on solving, reasoning or communication.

Learning and evaluation situations (LES)

The "Learning and evaluation situations" (LES), presented in the *Teaching Guide*, are grouped according to a common thematic thread; each focuses on a general field of instruction, a subject-specific competency and two cross-curricular competencies. The knowledge acquired through the sections helps to complete the tasks required in the LES.

REFERENCE

Located at the end of the *Student Book*, the "Reference" section contains several tools that support the student-learning process. It consists of two distinct parts.

The "Technology" part provides explanations pertaining to the main functions of a graphing calculator, the use of a spreadsheet program as well as the use of dynamic geometry software.

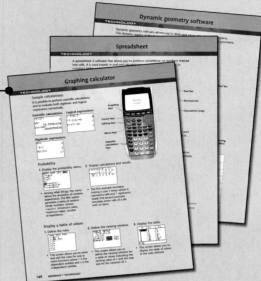

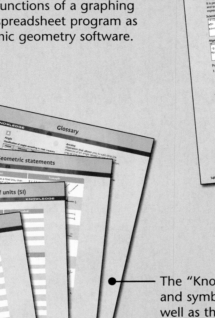

The "Knowledge" part presents notations and symbols used in the *Student Book* as well as those of the International System of Units (SI). Geometric statements are also listed. This part concludes with a glossary and an index.

ICONS

 Indicates that a worksheet is available in the *Teaching Guide*.

 Indicates that the activity can be performed in teams. Details on this topic are provided in the *Teaching Guide*.

 Indicates that some key features of subject-specific competency 1 are mobilized.

Indicates that some key features of subject-specific competency 2 are mobilized.

 Indicates that some key features of subject-specific competency 3 are mobilized.

VISI3N

Graphs

How should you connect the computers in a network to avoid data loss while minimizing the number of connections? How do you establish the minimum number of colours needed to colour the map of a continent if two bordering countries must be of different colours? How do you arrange the stages in the construction of a bridge so that the work is carried out as quickly as possible? In "Vision 3," you will analyze situations that can be represented using graphs. You will explore different types of graphs and learn how to translate and solve complex situations using graphs. Finally, you will use graphs to optimize various situations.

Arithmetic and algebra   **Geometry**   **Graphs**   **Probability**

- Representing and modelling a situation using a graph
- Directed graph and weighted graph
- Optimizing and making decisions
- Euler and Hamiltonian paths and circuits
- Tree diagram and critical path
- Coloured graph and chromatic number

LEARNING AND
EVALUATION
SITUATIONS

Transportation
networks

Chronicle of the
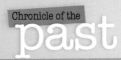

Claude Berge

In the
workplace

Performance-venue
technical directors

PRIOR LEARNING **1** Buying a car

Lea is negotiating the purchase of her first car from a dealership.

I'M CONSIDERING BUYING A CAR WITH A HYBRID OR A DIESEL ENGINE. THREE CATEGORIES INTEREST ME: THE SUB-COMPACT, THE COMPACT AND THE SEDAN.

UNLIKE THE OTHER TWO CATEGORIES, THE SEDAN ONLY COMES WITH A HYBRID ENGINE. ALL MODELS ARE AVAILABLE IN BLUE, RED, BLACK AND WHITE.

a. Complete the adjacent tree diagram.

b. How many characteristics must Lea decide upon before proceeding with the purchase?

c. How many different cars can Lea choose from?

d. If Lea chooses a car at random, what is the probability that she chooses a black hybrid?

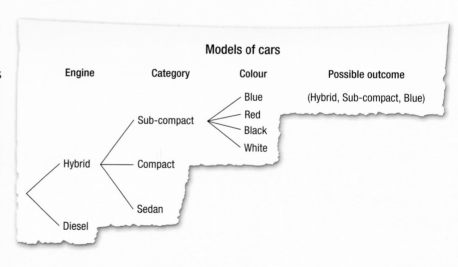

After taking possession of her car, Lea must go to the registration office. The network below shows the possible routes that she can take to get there.

e. From her house, how many different routes can she take to get to the registration office?

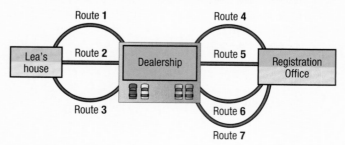

PRIOR LEARNING 2 The Euler relation

Leonhard Euler demonstrated that it is possible to determine the number of faces of a polyhedron based on the number of vertices and edges. The relation can be expressed as follows:

Number of faces = (number of edges) − (number of vertices) + 2

a. Complete the following table.

Polyhedron	Right triangular-based prism	Cube	Regular octagonal-based prism
Number of faces			
Number of edges			
Number of vertices			

b. Show that the Euler relation applies to these three polyhedrons.

c. How many vertices does a polyhedron with 8 faces and 12 edges have?

d. How many edges does a polyhedron with 11 faces and 11 vertices have?

e. Draw a polyhedron made up of:
   1) 10 vertices and 7 faces
   2) 8 faces and 14 edges

f. Verify whether the Euler relation applies to a right cylinder.

Leonhard Euler (1707-1783), of Swiss origin, is considered to be one of the greatest mathematicians of all time. A friend of the Bernoulli family, he lived in Germany and Russia for most of his life. In 1735, he became almost blind and compensated for this difficulty with his amazing memory and his mental calculation skills. Euler made important discoveries in the field of graph theory.

knowledge summary

TREE DIAGRAMS AND NETWORKS

An experiment with several steps can be represented using a tree diagram or a network. You can write the set of all the possible outcomes of an experiment with several steps in brace brackets where elements are separated by commas.

E.g.

Tree diagram

1) You must randomly choose one sweater out of 4, one pair of pants out of 3 and one coat out of 2.

Choice of sweater	Choice of pants	Choice of coat	Possible outcomes
	P_1	C_1	(S_1, P_1, C_1)
		C_2	(S_1, P_1, C_2)
S_1	P_2	C_1	(S_1, P_2, C_1)
		C_2	(S_1, P_2, C_2)
	P_3	C_1	(S_1, P_3, C_1)
		C_2	(S_1, P_3, C_2)
	P_1	C_1	(S_2, P_1, C_1)
		C_2	(S_2, P_1, C_2)
S_2	P_2	C_1	(S_2, P_2, C_1)
		C_2	(S_2, P_2, C_2)
	P_3	C_1	(S_2, P_3, C_1)
		C_2	(S_2, P_3, C_2)
	P_1	C_1	(S_3, P_1, C_1)
		C_2	(S_3, P_1, C_2)
S_3	P_2	C_1	(S_3, P_2, C_1)
		C_2	(S_3, P_2, C_2)
	P_3	C_1	(S_3, P_3, C_1)
		C_2	(S_3, P_3, C_2)
	P_1	C_1	(S_4, P_1, C_1)
		C_2	(S_4, P_1, C_2)
S_4	P_2	C_1	(S_4, P_2, C_1)
		C_2	(S_4, P_2, C_2)
	P_3	C_1	(S_4, P_3, C_1)
		C_2	(S_4, P_3, C_2)

Set of possible outcomes: $\{(S_1, P_1, C_1), (S_1, P_1, C_2), (S_1, P_2, C_1), \ldots, (S_4, P_3, C_2)\}$

2) You must determine the number of possible routes to travel from City **A** to City **C** through City **B**. There are three routes connecting City **A** and City **B** and two routes connecting City **B** and City **C**.

Network

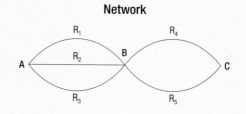

Set of possible outcomes: $\{(R_1, R_4), (R_1, R_5), (R_2, R_4), (R_2, R_5), (R_3, R_4), (R_3, R_5)\}$

POLYGON

A polygon is a plane figure formed by a closed, broken line.

In a polygon, the following is true:

- A vertex is the intersection point of two sides.
- Sides are adjacent if they have a common vertex.
- Angles are consecutive if they have a common side.

E.g.

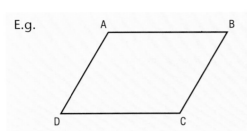

In quadrilateral ABCD, the following can be noted:

- $\overline{AB}$ and $\overline{AD}$ are adjacent sides.
- $\angle$ B and $\angle$ C are consecutive angles.

SOLID

A solid is a portion of space bounded by a closed surface.

E.g. 1) 2) 3) 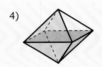 4) 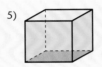 5) 6)

A solid can be described using faces, edges and vertices.

Face
A face is a plane or curved surface bounded by edges.

Edge
An edge is the line of intersection between two faces of a solid.

Vertex
A vertex is a point common to at least two edges of a solid.

E.g. This solid has
7 faces,
15 edges,
10 vertices.

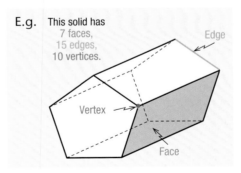

Polyhedron

A polyhedron is a solid whose plane faces are polygons.

E.g. 1) 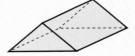 2) 3)

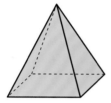

knowledge in action

1 For each of the polyhedrons below, determine:

   1) the number of vertices   2) the number of edges   3) the number of faces

a) 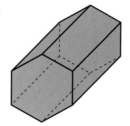   b)   c)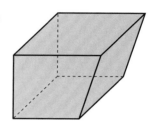

2 For each case, determine the set of all possible outcomes.

a) A marble is chosen at random from a bag containing a red marble, a yellow marble and a green marble. A card is then drawn at random from a deck of 52 cards. The colour of the marble and that of the card (red or black) are noted.

b) Two dice numbered 1 to 6 are rolled, and the sum of the results is noted.

c) A coin is tossed and a die numbered 1 to 6 is rolled. The two results are noted.

d) A number that is divisible by 7 is chosen at random from the 50 first natural numbers.

3 Josephine uses public transport to get to work. From her home to Stop **A**, there are 3 bus routes she can take. From Stop **A** to Stop **B**, there are 4 bus routes she can take. From Stop **B** to her workplace, there are 2 bus routes she can take.

a) Represent this situation using a network.

b) How many different routes can Josephine take to get to work?

A tramway connects New York City's Manhattan to Roosevelt Island. Built in 1976 as a temporary public transport solution for the residents of the island, the tramway remained in service after a subway connection opened in the late 1980s. It is the only commuter aerial tramway in North America.

4 A female rabbit gives birth to baby rabbits. The babies can be male or female, have red eyes or brown eyes and have cream-coloured or black fur.

a) Represent this situation using a tree diagram.

b) How many different baby rabbits can this female rabbit give birth to?

c) What is the probability of this rabbit giving birth to a baby with red eyes and black fur?

5 Draw a pyramid that has:

a) 6 faces b) 5 vertices c) 10 edges

6 For each of the following net polyhedrons, indicate:

1) the number of vertices of the polyhedron 2) the number of edges of the polyhedron

a) 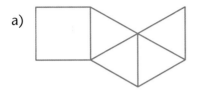 b) 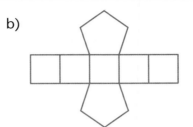 c)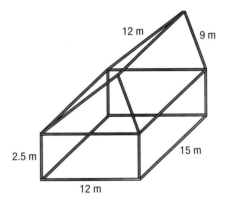

7 The adjacent illustration represents the frame of a metal structure.

a) How many beams does this frame have?

b) What is the total length of the beams that make up this frame?

c) In how many locations do:

1) exactly 3 beams meet?

2) exactly 4 beams meet?

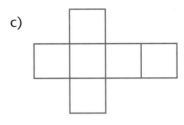

8 The tree diagram below presents all the different snowboards available for purchase in a store.

a) How many characteristics does a snowboard have?

b) How many different snowboards does this store sell?

c) How many different snowboards:

1) belong to the freestyle category?

2) have plate bindings?

3) are short and have soft bindings?

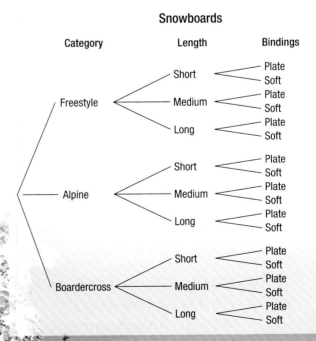

9 Draw the net of each of the following solids.

a)

b)
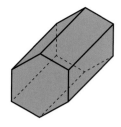

c)
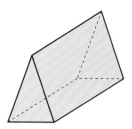

10 For each of the polygons below, do the following:

  1) Indicate the number of vertices.
  2) Determine the number of diagonals that can be drawn.
  3) Identify a pair of adjacent sides.
  4) Identify two consecutive angles.

a)
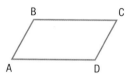

b)
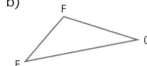

c)
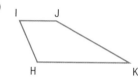

d)

11 The code for an electronic lock is composed of four characters. The first character is a consonant, the second is an even number between 0 and 9, the third is a vowel, and the last is an odd number between 0 and 9. How many different codes could this lock have?

12 The diagram below illustrates the routes that connect different cities. How many routes must be added for each city to have a direct road link with every other city?

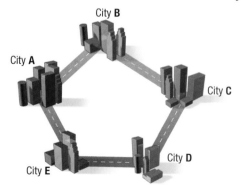

13 To help clients visualize different hair styles, a hairdresser uses a computer program that allows 12 hair cuts and 8 colours to be applied to a virtual character and gives the option of adding natural hair extensions. How many different ways can the virtual character's hair be styled?

14 In a particular section of a zoo, there are elephants, gazelles and macaques.
The tree diagram below presents some characteristics of these animals.

Zoo animals

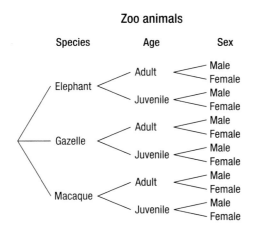

For some species of wild animals, reproduction in captivity is problematic because the living conditions in their natural habitat cannot be recreated in a controlled environment.

A person takes a picture in this section of the zoo.

a) How many different animals can be photographed if species, age and sex are taken into account?

b) Of the set of possible outcomes, how many pictures show:

1) an adult?

2) an adult macaque?

3) a male elephant?

15 Illustrate a solid composed of:

a) 0 edges and 0 vertices   b) 2 edges and 0 vertices

16 Diego chooses three classes from the following: karate, diving, hip hop and cycling.

a) Illustrate this situation using a tree diagram.

b) From how many different possibilities can Diego choose?

17 The following options are available for the publication of a comic book:

- The cover can be cardboard or plastic.
- It can be printed in two, three or five colours.
- The paper can be matte or glossy.

a) How many different publications can be produced?

b) Considering that a cardboard cover costs $6 and a plastic cover $10, that printing in two colours costs $5, in three colours, $8, and in five colours, $10, and that matte paper costs $8 and glossy paper, $14, determine the possible combinations that generate the same publication cost.

PROBLEM The Montréal Metro system

Montréal's Metro system is composed of 4 lines and 68 stations. A specific colour is associated with each line: orange, blue, green and yellow. When travelling on the Metro, you can change lines at transfer stations. The adjacent map shows Montreal's Metro system:

Transfer stations
- Jean-Talon
- Snowdon
- Berri-UQAM
- Lionel-Groulx

Terminal
- Yellow line: Longueuil-Université-de-Sherbrooke Berri-UQAM
- Orange line: Montmorency and Côte-Vertu
- Blue line: Saint-Michel and Snowdon
- Green line: Angrignon and Honoré-Beaugrand

Five people are meeting at the Snowdon station. The following information provided is about their trips:

- None of the people can travel through the same station twice, except for transfer stations.
- Antoine leaves from the Montmorency station, travels through only one transfer station and arrives at his destination.
- Chloe leaves from the Honoré-Beaugrand station, travels through two transfer stations and arrives at her destination.
- Dominic leaves from the Longueuil-Université-de-Sherbrooke station, travels through a minimum number of transfer stations and arrives at his destination.
- Julie leaves from the Côte-Vertu station and arrives at her destination.
- Veronica leaves from the Angrignon station, travels through at least two transfer stations and arrives at her destination.

Determine all the possible routes that each person could have taken.

ACTIVITY **1** The United Arab Emirates

In recent years, the United Arab Emirates have undertaken several large-scale tourism projects. The World project, whose construction began in 2003, is one of these unprecedented undertakings. This archipelago of 300 artificial islands copies the representation of a map of the world and is located in the Persian Gulf, off the Emirate of Dubai. Boats are used to travel between these islands.

Aerial view of The World project

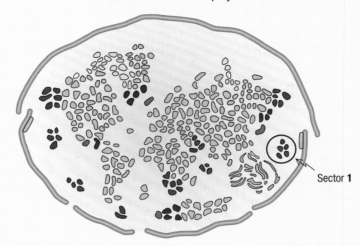

Sector **1**

Illustration of the possible boat routes in Sector **1**

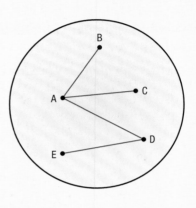

a. In the illustration of Sector **1**, what is represented by:

1) the points?   2) the lines?

b. Which islands can a person get to directly from:

1) Island **A**?   2) Island **D**?   3) Island **E**?

c. Is it possible to reach any island in Sector **1** from any other island in the sector? Explain your answer.

d. In this sector, how many boat routes should be added to allow direct travel from any island to any other island?

The city of Dubai is known for the scale of its development projects, including the Dubai Marina, a waterway project surrounded by residential buildings and hotels built in the desert.

GRAPH

A **graph** corresponds to a set of elements and the links that exist between these elements.

In the graphical representation of a graph, note the following:

- The points, called **vertices**, correspond to the elements of the set and the lines, called **edges**, correspond to the links that exist between the elements.
- The vertices are generally identified by a lowercase letter, an uppercase letter, a number or a word.
- An edge is generally named by combining the letters that identify its endpoints in any order.

E.g. 1) In the graph below, note the following:

- Points A, B, C, D and E are vertices.
- A-B, B-C and C-D are edges.

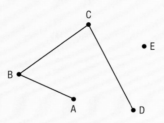

2) In the graph below, note the following:

- 1, 2 and 3 are vertices.
- 1-2 and 1-3 are edges.

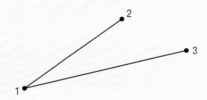

The following characteristics can be associated with a graph:

- The **order** of a graph corresponds to the number of vertices.
- The **degree of a vertex** corresponds to the number of edges that meet at that vertex.
- Two vertices connected by the same edge are **adjacent**.
- Edges that connect the same vertices are **parallel** and are generally written using numbers in parentheses.
- An edge that connects a vertex to itself is called a **loop**.

E.g. In the graph below, note the following:
- The order of the graph is 5.
- Vertex k is of degree 2 and vertex m is of degree 3.
- Vertices m and p are adjacent.
- Edge k(1)-j is parallel to edge k(2)-j.
- Edge m-m is a loop.

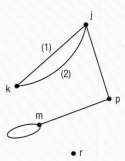

CONNECTED GRAPH

A graph is considered to be connected if any vertex is linked, directly or not, to all other vertices of the graph.

E.g. 1) Connected graph

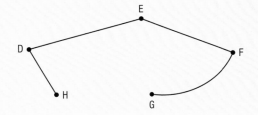

2) Disconnected graph

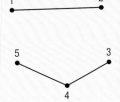

COMPLETE GRAPH

A graph is considered to be complete if each vertex is directly linked to every other vertex.

E.g. 1) Complete graph

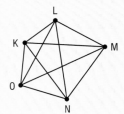

2) Incomplete graph

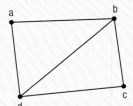

1 For each of the following graphs, determine:

1) the order   2) the number of edges   3) the degree of each vertex

a)
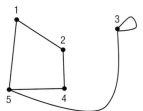

b)
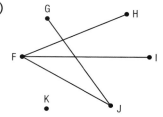

2 Based on the adjacent graph, explain why the following statements are false.

a) The order of the graph is 6.

b) The degree of vertex 4 is 2.

c) Vertex 5 is adjacent to vertices 1, 2, 3 and 4.

d) The graph is complete.

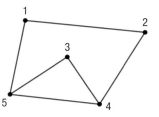

3 Identify the edges of each of the following graphs.

a)
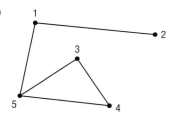

b)
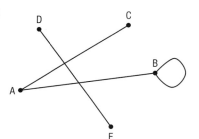

c)
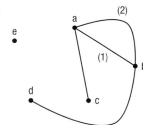

4 For each case, indicate whether or not the graph is connected. If it is not, identify an edge that could be added to make the graph connected.

a)
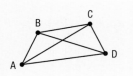

b)
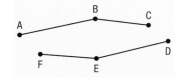

c)
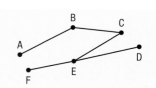

d)
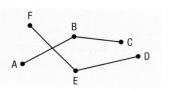

e)
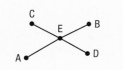

f)
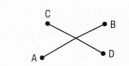

5 Among the graphs below, identify those that could represent the same situation.

A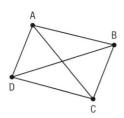

B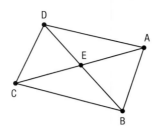

C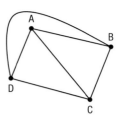

D

E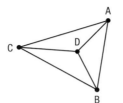

F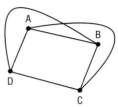

6 For each case, indicate whether or not the graph is complete. If it is not, identify the edges that must be added to make the graph complete.

a)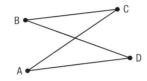

b)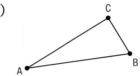

c)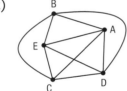

d)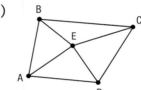

7 The graph below represents the flight routes between different airports.

Flight routes between different airports

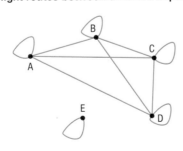

In Canada, the Transportation Safety Board is responsible for investigating aviation-related incidents.

a) For each airport, identify the different non-stop flights that are offered.

b) What is particular about Airport **E**?

c) There is a plan to offer travellers the possibility of getting to any airport from any other airport, with or without a stopover. What must be done to offer travellers this possibility?

8 For each of the graphs described below, provide:

1) its graphical representation
2) its order
3) the degree of each of its vertices

		Set of vertices	Set of edges
a)	Graph **A**	{a, b, c, d, e}	{a-a, a-c, b-d, b-c, a-d, d-d}
b)	Graph **B**	{1, 2, 3, 4}	{1-2, 2-3, 3-3, 1-4, 1-1}
c)	Graph **C**	{V, W, X, Y, Z}	{X-W, Y-Z, Y-W, W-W, X-X}

9 The following graph illustrates the friendship links that connect the people in a group.

a) Who has a friendship link with everyone else?

b) Who has friendship links with only two other people in the group?

c) 1) How many new relationships must be established for each person to have friendship links with every other person in the group?

2) If all the friendship links are created, what type of graph would allow this situation to be represented graphically?

Friendship links among people in a group

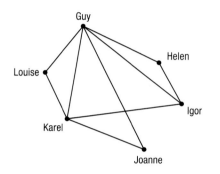

10 Marguerite and Gabrielle have created graphs to represent the route they each take to get from home to school. What do you notice?

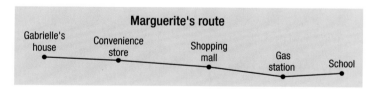

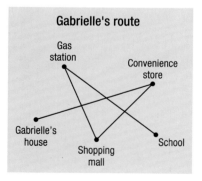

11 Construct a graph whose edges connect the words from set L below that have at least three consecutive letters in common.

L = {vertices, kinship, tickle, running, arctic, nicely, graph, kicking, notice, nothing}

12 The adjacent graph presents a car manufacturer's models. An edge connects two models if they have at least one part in common.

a) How many models have at least one part in common with Model **C**?

b) Which models have at least one part in common with each other?

c) Which model does not have a part in common with any other model?

Car models offered by a manufacturer

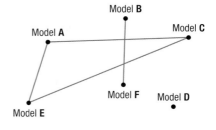

13 In a karate competition, participants can face each other if the difference in their ages does not exceed 2 years. Participants are between the ages of 12 and 18.

a) Using a graph, illustrate the different match possibilities.

b) Which age categories offer the most match possibilities?

c) What are the possible ages of a participant if he or she cannot face a 15-year-old participant?

d) What are the possible ages of a participant if he or she can face an 18-year-old participant?

14 **GEOGRAPHY** Using the map of Canada below, do the following:

a) For the set of provinces and territories, construct a graph representing the relationship "… has a common land border with…."

b) Which province or territory has the most common land borders with others?

c) Which provinces or territories have only one common land border?

d) Which province or territory has no common land borders with others?

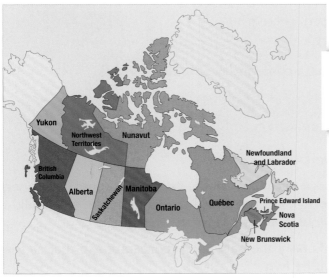

On April 1, 1999, Nunavut was recognized as one of the three territories under the Canadian Constitution. Although its boundaries have existed since 1993, it was part of the Northwest Territories.

15 PANGEA According to the continental drift theory, a large continent called Pangea broke apart millions of years ago and, over time, formed the current continents. Below is a representation of this situation:

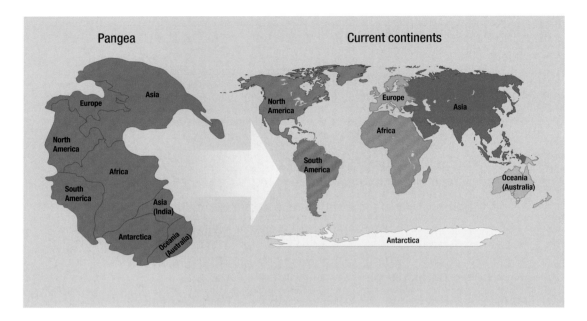

Which current continent had the most common borders with the other continents in the time of Pangea?

16 Carole is working with Annie, Bernard, Diane and Elizabeth on the publication of a novel. Annie, Diane and Elizabeth work together.

a) Using a graph, illustrate the working relationships between these people.

b) At work, who has the fewest interactions with others?

c) How many working relationships must be added for all the members of the team to work with every other member?

17 The following is information about a company's computer network:

> • Computers: {A, B, C, D, E, F}
> • Network connections: {A-C, C-B, D-E, D-F, B-A}

a) Illustrate this computer network using a graph.

b) According to the installation specifications, all the computers must be connected to one another directly or indirectly. Suggest a possible modification that could be made to the network that would allow these specifications to be met.

c) Following a computer system crash, the network is reorganized so that all the computers are connected two by two.

1) Using a graph, illustrate this new network.

2) To how many computers is each computer connected?

18 For each of the following situations, show that at least one person has not provided the correct information.

    a) Over the course of an event, 8 people dance. At the end of the evening, they claim to have danced, respectively, with 7, 6, 5, 4, 4, 3, 3 and 1 different persons.

    b) One day, 7 people ski together. They meet at the end of the day and claim to have skied with 6, 6, 5, 4, 4, 3 and 3 different people.

19 The following graph illustrates a building's points of access.

Accesses to a building's rooms and hallways

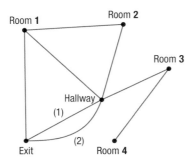

The White House, in Washington, is open to the public for guided tours. However, security surrounding this building and the grounds of the President of the United State's official residence has been strengthened over the years with air defense measures and widened protection zones.

    a) How many points of access does the hallway have?

    b) A security standard stipulates that each room must have at least two points of access. Which edge must be added to the graph for the building to comply with the standard?

    c) Draw the plan of a building that meets this standard.

20 In a new electrical installation, six devices must be wired to an electrical box. Construct the graph that illustrates each of the situations described below.

    a) Each device must be directly connected to the electrical box, and the number of electrical wires must be kept to a minimum.

    b) Each device must be directly wired to the electrical box and connected to only one other device with an electrical wire.

    c) Each device must be directly wired to the electrical box and connected to each of the other devices.

Lightning is a discharge of electricity that results from the build-up of static electricity among clouds or between clouds and the ground.

This section is related to LES 8.

PROBLEM Satellite communication

Satellites allow for almost instantaneous communication from one end of the planet to the other. The transmission of a signal sometimes requires the use of several satellites.

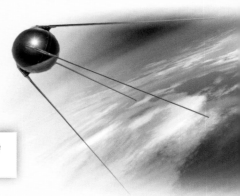

On October 4, 1957, the USSR launched the first artificial satellite, *Sputnik 1*, into orbit.

The following graph represents the possible communication channels of a satellite system.

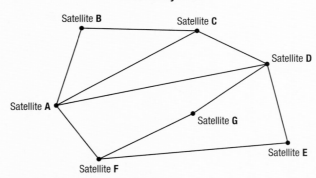

Satellite system

Satellite **B** Satellite **C**

Satellite **D**

Satellite **A**

Satellite **G**

Satellite **E**

Satellite **F**

A signal used to verify the efficiency of the satellite system has the following characteristics:
- The signal travels through each of the communication channels only once.
- The signal can be received and transmitted more than once by the same satellite.

Identify at least three channels that allow the signal to verify the efficiency of this satellite system.

The Global Positioning System (GPS) makes use of some thirty satellites that travel in different orbits and use triangulation to determine and communicate a precise geographical position within a few metres.

During a high-altitude ascent, climbers must usually climb up and down certain parts of the mountain several times in order to acclimatize themselves to the altitude. The map below presents the trails and camps that allow a mountain to be climbed.

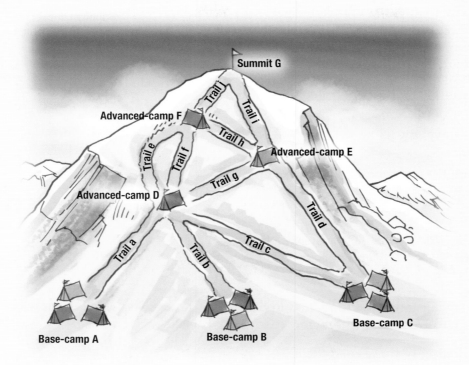

a. What is the minimum number of trails a climber can take to reach the summit, starting from:

1) Base-camp **A**?   2) Base-camp **B**?   3) Base-camp **C**?

b. A climber located at Base-camp **C** wants to reach Summit **G** without climbing downwards. Identify all the routes the climber can take.

c. Starting from Base-camp **C**, the support team wants to deliver supplies to every second base camp, to each advanced camp and to the summit while travelling through each of these locations only once. Is this possible? Explain your answer.

d. A climber located at Base-camp **A** wants to take every trail once only and finish at Base-camp **B**. Is this possible? Explain your answer.

Buddhist prayer flags at the foot of Mount Everest. These prayer flags, called *loungta*, flutter in the wind in regions where Buddhism is practiced, namely in Nepal, Tibet and Bhutan. Each colour of these small rectangular pieces of cloth corresponds to an element: red symbolizes fire, yellow symbolizes earth, blue symbolizes water, green symbolizes wood, and white symbolizes iron.

ACTIVITY 2 Just-in-time production

Just-in-time production is a production management method that allows a company to minimize the storage of raw materials or products it manufactures. Close coordination between the company's suppliers, transporters and distributors allows this method to be used.

A company whose manufacturing plant is located in East-Angus distributes its products to the region shown in the adjacent illustration.

a. Identify a route that a truck can take to make a round-trip delivery from the plant to Asbestos:

1) if it can travel the same road twice

2) if it cannot travel the same road twice

b. Is it possible for a delivery truck to leave the plant, travel through each city just once and return to the plant? Explain your answer.

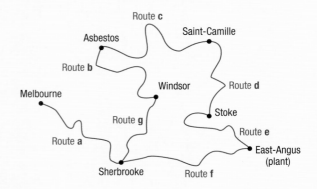

Distribution network of a company's products

The adjacent map illustrates the road links in the region after the construction of three new roads.

c. After the addition of these roads, is it possible to identify a route that meets the conditions stated in **b.**? Explain your answer.

d. Identify a route that allows a delivery truck to leave the plant, travel along every road only once and return to the plant.

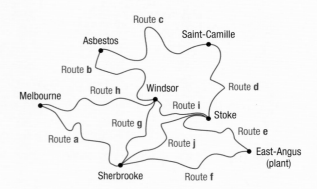

New distribution network

The "just-in-time" principle is of Japanese origin. The limited storage space available to businesses in that country forced the Japanese to develop an immediate delivery system for manufactured products.

PATHS AND CIRCUITS

In a graph, a **path** is established when you can travel from one vertex to another by following the edges.

- The **length** of a path corresponds to the number of times you travel from one vertex to another.

- The **distance** between two vertices A and B, written d(A, B), corresponds to the length of the shortest path that connects the two vertices.

E.g. In the adjacent graph, note the following: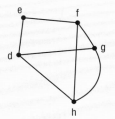
- d-e-f and e-f-g-h-g-d are paths.
- The length of path d-g-f-e is 3 and that of path g-d-e-d-g-h is 5.
- d(f, h) = 1 and d(h, e) = 2.

In a graph, a **circuit** is a path that starts and ends at the same vertex.

E.g. In the adjacent graph, A-B-E-B-A and D-C-E-B-E-A-D are circuits.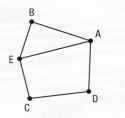

Simple path and simple circuit

A path is said to be **simple** if it contains no repeated edges.

E.g. In the adjacent graph, A-B-C-D and F-E-C-B-A-D-C are simple paths.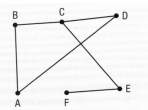

A circuit is said to be **simple** if it contains no repeated edges.

E.g. In the adjacent graph, 2-3-1-2 is a simple circuit.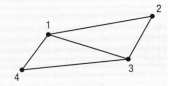

Euler path and Euler circuit

An **Euler path** is a path that visits every edge in a connected graph just once.

An **Euler circuit** is an Euler path that starts and ends at the same vertex.

A graph contains an Euler path if the following is true:

- All the vertices are of even degree. This path starts at any vertex and ends at the same vertex. It is considered to be an Euler circuit.
- There are exactly 2 vertices of odd degree. This path starts at a vertex of an odd degree and ends at another vertex of an odd degree.

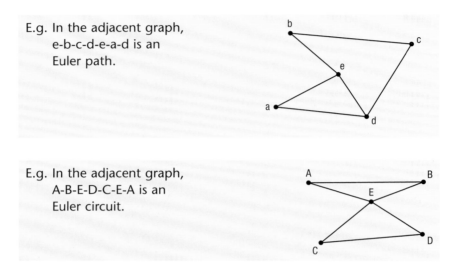

E.g. In the adjacent graph,
e-b-c-d-e-a-d is an
Euler path.

E.g. In the adjacent graph,
A-B-E-D-C-E-A is an
Euler circuit.

Hamiltonian path and Hamiltonian circuit

A **Hamiltonian path** is a simple path that visits every vertex of a connected graph only once.

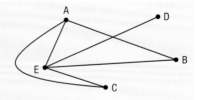

E.g. In the adjacent graph,
D-E-C-A-B is a Hamiltonian
path.

A **Hamiltonian circuit** is a simple circuit that visits every vertex of a connected graph only once.

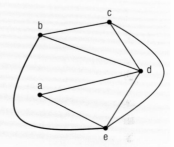

E.g. In the adjacent graph,
a-e-b-c-d-a is a
Hamiltonian circuit.

1 For the graph below, do the following:

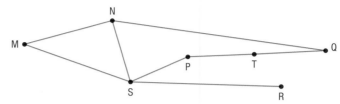

a) Identify a simple circuit.

b) Identify a simple path connecting vertex R to vertex Q.

c) Determine d(R, Q).

d) Determine the length of path M-N-S-M-N-Q.

2 For each case, do the following:

1) Indicate if the graph contains an Euler path, an Euler circuit or neither one.

2) If the graph contains an Euler path or an Euler circuit, identify the path or circuit.

a)

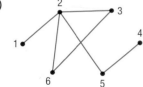

b)

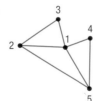

c)

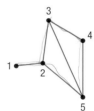

d)

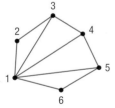

e)

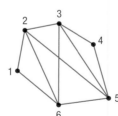

f)

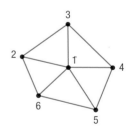

3 Among the following statements, identify those that are false and explain why.

A A circuit is also a path.

B A simple path is also a simple circuit.

C The distance between two vertices is always equal to the length of a path that connects these two vertices.

D A simple circuit is also a path.

E A Hamiltonian path necessarily includes an Euler path.

4 For each case, do the following:

1) Indicate whether the graph contains a Hamiltonian path, a Hamiltonian circuit or neither one.

2) If the graph contains a Hamiltonian path or a Hamiltonian circuit, identify the path or circuit.

a)
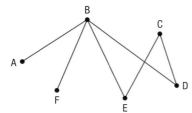

b)
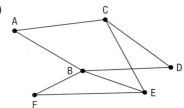

c)
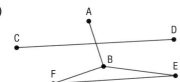

d)
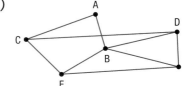

e)
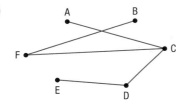

f)
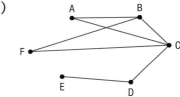

5 For each case, construct a graph using the following criteria.

a) a connected graph of order 6 that contains two simple circuits

b) a graph of order 5 composed of 4 edges and containing a Hamiltonian path

c) a graph of order 7 composed of 9 edges and containing an Euler path

d) a graph of order 5 that contains an Euler circuit and wherein the degree of every vertex is greater than 2

6 For each of the following graphs, identify, if possible, an Euler path.

a)
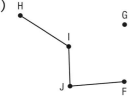

b)

c)
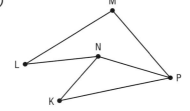

7 For each of the following graphs, identify, if possible, an Euler circuit.

a)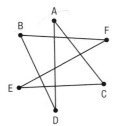

b)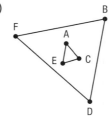

c)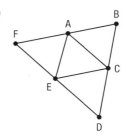

8 For each of the graphs described below, do the following:

1) Provide its graphical representation.

2) Identify, if possible, an Euler path or an Euler circuit.

		Set of vertices	Set of edges
a)	Graph **A**	{a, b, c, d, e}	{a-b, a-d, a-e, b-b, b-c, c-d, e-e}
b)	Graph **B**	{1, 2, 3, 4}	{1-2, 1-3, 1-4, 3-2, 4-3, 4-2}
c)	Graph **C**	{A, B, C, D, E}	{A-B, D-B, D(1)-C, A-E, E-D, C(2)-D}

9 THE PETERSEN GRAPH In 1898, Julius Petersen drew the adjacent graph for the first time. Based on the graph, provide:

a) d(A, C)

b) d(G, J)

c) a simple path of length 4

d) a simple circuit of length 9

e) the length of path A-F-H-J-E-D

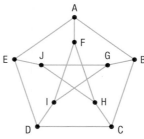

Danish mathematician Julius Petersen (1839-1910)

10 To send a signal from one user to another, a cellular telephone company uses many antennas. The following graph presents its network of antennas.

A cellular telephone company's antenna network

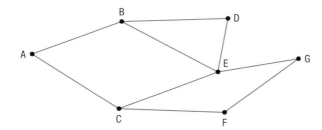

A technician tests network reliability by emitting a signal that starts from Antenna **C** and must travel the entire network without using the same transmission line twice. Identify this transmission path.

11 **KÖNIGSBERG** In the 18th century, the city of Königsberg had 7 bridges that connected the city's two banks and two islands. The adjacent illustration represents this situation:

a) Represent this situation using a graph.

b) Is it possible to visit the city by crossing each of the 7 bridges just once? Explain your answer.

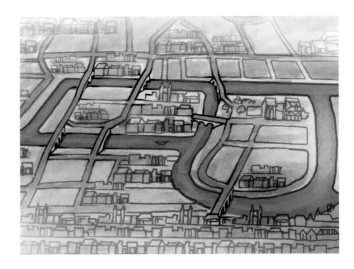

12 The adjacent graph illustrates the possible points of access between a museum's various exhibition rooms. Considering that the visit starts in the Pharaohs-room, suggest a way to visit each of the rooms once and then return to the original room.

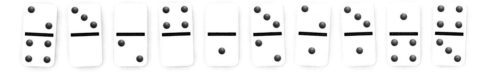

A museum's exhibition rooms

Middle ages · Prehistory · Babylonians · Pharaohs · Mayas · Great explorers · Renaissance

13 **DOMINOES** A domino has two numbers that are represented by dots. One of the variations of the game of dominoes consists of laying out the dominoes so that two identical numbers from two different dominoes are touching. The following are the 10 dominoes picked by an individual.

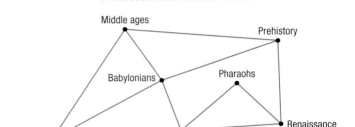

a) Represent this situation using a graph whose five vertices correspond to the numbers 0, 1, 2, 3 and 4 indicated on the dominoes and wherein each edge connects two numbers on the same domino.

b) Explain how it would be possible to lay out these 10 dominoes according to the rules of the game.

c) If the individual picks the additional 5 dominoes below, is it possible to lay out these 15 dominoes according to the rules of the game? Explain your answer.

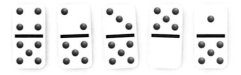

14 The adjacent graph represents the waterways through which a boat can navigate to supply offshore Oil rigs **A**, **B**, **C**, **D** and **E**. Identify a route that that starts and finishes at Port **F** and allows the ship to dock at each oil rig a single time.

Network of offshore oil rigs

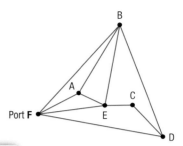

After an oil reservoir has been fully exploited, some oil rigs are reused as space launchers.

15 In the adjacent graph, each edge corresponds to a street in a residential neighbourhood and each vertex to the intersection of two streets.

Streets in a residential area

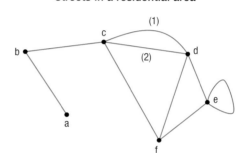

a) In this context, what does the loop represent at Intersection **e**?

b) Identify a route that allows snow to be cleared from all these streets by taking each street just once.

c) Considering that the annual snow removal for a single street costs $2,000, determine the minimum annual cost of snow for this area.

d) If a road is built between Intersections **a** and **f**, at what intersection should snow removal begin? Explain your answer.

16 THE *ROUTE VERTE* The *Route verte* project, which was launched in 1995, consisted of developing over 4300 km of bicycle-paths throughout Québec. The following graph represents 11 bicycle-paths connecting 10 Québec regions.

Bicycle path network

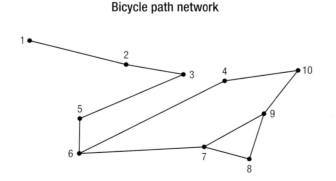

Region
1. Abitibi-Témiscamingue
2. Outaouais
3. Laurentides
4. Lanaudière
5. Laval
6. Montréal
7. Montérégie
8. Eastern Townships
9. Central Québec
10. Mauricie

a) A cyclist takes the *Route verte* to travel from Central Québec to Montréal. What is the minimum number of bicycle-paths that must be taken?

b) Is it possible for this cyclist to take six different bicycle-paths and return to the starting point? Explain your answer.

17 Consider the two adjacent graphs:

a) Can these two graphs represent the same situation? Explain your answer.

b) Can it be stated that Graph ② contains an Euler circuit because the degree of each vertex is even? Explain your answer.

c) Identify an Euler circuit in Graph ①.

d) In Graph ②, identify an edge that could be added to create an Euler path.

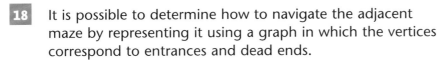

Graph ①   Graph ②

18 It is possible to determine how to navigate the adjacent maze by representing it using a graph in which the vertices correspond to entrances and dead ends.

a) Represent this maze using a graph.

b) Identify the path that allows you to navigate the maze from the starting point to the finish without backtracking.

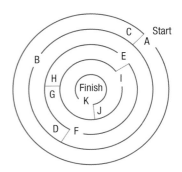

19 The graph below presents tourist attractions in Québec City as well as various ways of travelling from one place to another.

Québec City Tourist Attractions

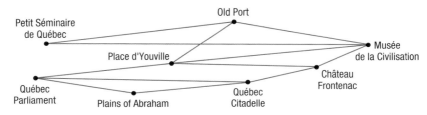

a) 1) Suggest a route that starts at the Château Frontenac, ends at the Musée de la Civilisation and allows each tourist attraction to be visited just once.

2) Determine the number of movements made on this route.

b) A person would rather start at the Musée de la Civilisation, end at the Château Frontenac, and visit each tourist attraction just once. How should the suggested route be modified?

c) Suggest a route that starts and ends at the Plains of Abraham and allows each of the other tourist attractions to be visited just once.

Place d'Youville was named in honour of Marguerite d'Youville, who founded the Order of Sisters of Charity of Montréal in 1737.

SECTION 3.3 Weighted graphs and directed graphs

This section is related to LES 7 and 8.

PROBLEM Industrial research and development

Before a new product is introduced to the market, companies carry out research and generally build one or more prototypes. Various research and development models help determine a product's production costs.

The graphs below present a company's two possible research and development models.

Company research and development

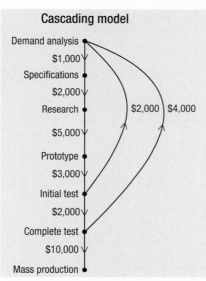

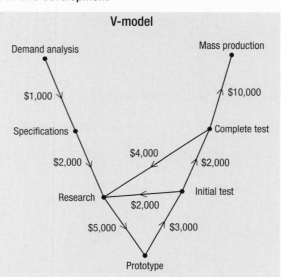

For each of these models, each number corresponds to the amount that must be invested before moving on to the next step.

Which model should this company adopt in order to minimize its costs?

Computer analysts sometimes illustrate a concept to be programmed using charts, tables or graphs. An analyst is perfecting a program whose function is to recognize the multiples of certain numbers. Below is a representation of this situation:

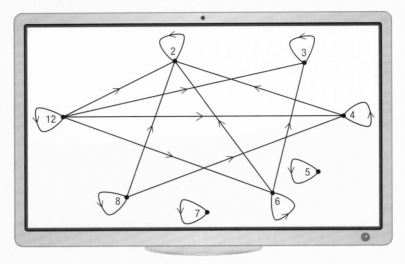

a. In this context, what does an arrow signify?

b. Is the direction of the arrow important? Explain your answer.

c. Why does each of the graph's vertices have a loop?

d. Using the graph, show in two different ways that 12 is a multiple of 3.

e. The computer analyst begins the representation of the relation "... is divisible by ..." using the graph below. Complete this representation.

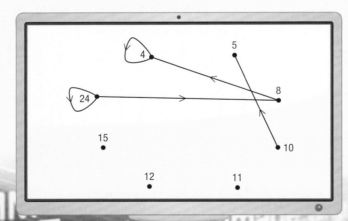

The HTML computer language is used to create Web pages and resulted from a project launched by American computer specialist Charles Goldfarb (1974).

ACTIVITY 2 Snowmobiling

In Québec, there are over 35 000 km of developed trails that can be used for snowmobiling. The graph below shows the trails that connect some cities in the Chaudière-Appalaches region. The value associated with each edge corresponds to the length (in km) of the trail.

Snowmobile trails in the Chaudière-Appalaches region

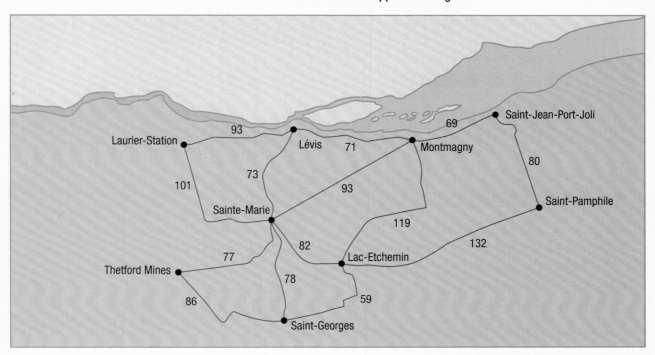

a. Determine the number of kilometres covered by a snowmobiler who travels the following routes:

1) Lac-Etchemin, Sainte-Marie, Lévis

2) Thetford Mines, Saint-Georges, Lac-Etchemin, Saint-Pamphile

b. A snowmobiler wants to travel from Saint-Jean-Port-Joli to Saint-Georges.

1) Identify all the possible routes that include three different trails.

2) How many kilometres make up each of these routes?

3) Which of these routes is the shortest?

c. 1) Identify all the possible routes between Saint-Pamphile and Laurier-Station that include three or four trails.

2) Which of these routes is the shortest?

The snowmobile was invented by Quebecker Joseph-Armand Bombardier (1907-1964).

TREE

A tree is a connected graph with no simple circuits.

E.g. 1) The following graph is a tree.

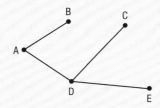

2) The following graph is not a tree because A-B-C-D-A is a simple circuit.

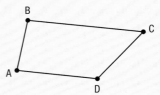

DIRECTED GRAPH

A directed graph is a graph in which a direction is attributed to each edge using an arrow. These edges are called arcs. In a directed graph, note the following:

> Arc A-B starts at vertex A and ends at vertex B. Arc B-A starts at vertex B and ends at vertex A.

- A **path** is a sequence of consecutive arcs that may or may not repeat.
- A **circuit** is a path that begins and ends at the same vertex.
- A path or circuit is **simple** if it contains no repeated arcs.

E.g. In the adjacent directed graph:
- D-E, F-D and G-F are arcs.
- F-D-E is a path.
- G-F-D(1)-G is a circuit.

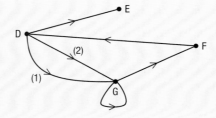

WEIGHTED GRAPH

A weighted graph is a graph, directed or not, in which a weight is attributed to each arc or to each edge. In a weighted graph, the **weight** of a path corresponds to the sum of the weights of the arcs or edges that make up the path.

E.g. In the adjacent graph:
- The weight of edge C-E is 4.
- The weight of path A-D-E-C is $9 + 8 + 4 = 21$.

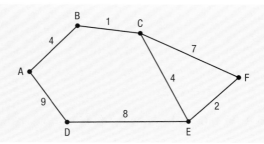

1 In the adjacent graph, do the following:

a) Identify a path of length 4.

b) Identify a simple circuit of length 3.

c) Does path A-E-D exist?
   Explain your answer.

d) What is the length of path:
   1) A-B-C-A-D-E?   2) A-D-E-D?

e) Determine:
   1) d(A, C)   2) d(E, C)

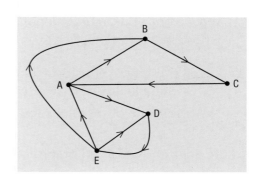

2 a) For each of the graphs below, determine:

   1) the sum of the degrees of the vertices   2) the number of edges

Graph ①

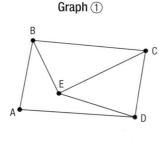

Graph ②

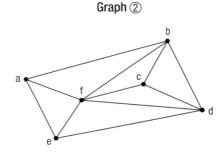

Graph ③

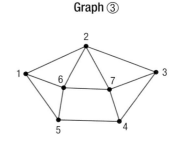

b) Formulate a conjecture regarding the answers determined in **a)**.

3 The graph below is weighted and directed.

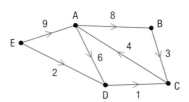

a) Determine the weight of path:
   1) E-D-C-A-D   2) B-C-A-D   3) E-A-B-C

b) 1) Identify all the simple paths going from vertex E to vertex B.

   2) Of the paths identified in **b) 1)**, which has the smallest weight?

4 Based on the adjacent graph, determine:

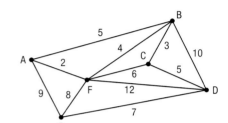

a) the weight of path A-B-C-F

b) the weight of circuit C-D-E-F-C

c) the weight of a circuit of length 3
   whose initial vertex is vertex A

d) 1) all the simple circuits of length 4
      whose initial vertex is vertex C

   2) which one of the paths found in **d) 1)** has the maximum weight

5 In the adjacent weighted graph, calculate:

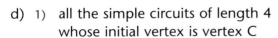

a) the weight of path A-B-C-D

b) the weight of path B-F-C-D

c) d(A, D)

d) d(B, D)

6 The table below provides information about a weighted graph whose vertices are V, W, X and Y. Draw this graph.

Edge	Weight of edge
X-W	5
W-Y	6
Y-V	8
V-X	9
X-Y	2

7 In the weighted graph below, does the length of path A-B-C-D correspond to the weight of path A-B-C-D? Explain your answer.

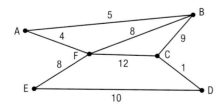

A constellation is a group of stars in the celestial vault that are relatively close and which were connected with imaginary lines to give them an imaginary form. The International Astronomical Union (IAU) has divided the sky into 88 officially recognized constellations.

8 In the graph below, remove edges in order to obtain a tree in which the maximum distance from vertex F to each of the other vertices is 2.

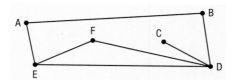

9 Draw a graph with vertices A, B, C, D and E and arcs A-A, A-C, B-D, B-C, A-D and D-D.

10 In the course of a job, some tasks must be carried out before others, and some can be carried out simultaneously. The table below identifies the tasks to be completed during a job as well as the prior required tasks.

Carrying out a job

Task	Prior tasks
A	None
B	A
C	A
D	B
E	A and B
F	C
G	D, E and F

a) Represent this situation using a directed graph.

b) What is the last task to be carried out for this job?

c) Determine the distance from A to G.

11 For each case, determine the number of edges that must be added to or removed from the graph in order to obtain a tree.

a)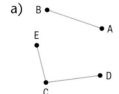

b)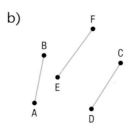

c)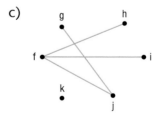

d)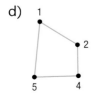

e)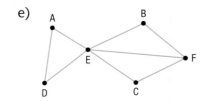

f)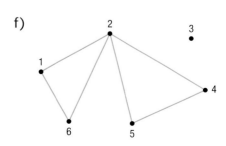

12 The graph below illustrates the results of the matches held at a soccer tournament. An arc connects Team **A** to Team **B** if Team **A** won against Team **B**. The weight attributed to each arc corresponds to the number of goals scored by the winning team.

Matches held at a soccer tournament

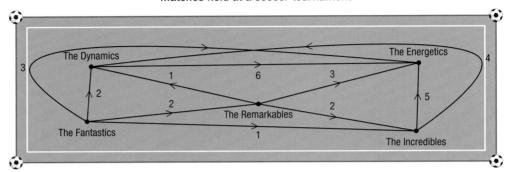

Which team won the tournament if the following is taken into account:

a) the greatest number of victories?

b) the total number of goals scored?

13 The graph below illustrates the time (in min) that it takes to walk from one bus stop to another.

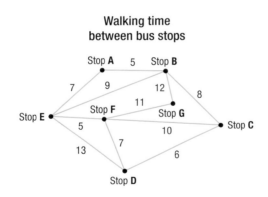

Walking time between bus stops

Double-decker buses were introduced in the mid-1950s and are now used as sightseeing buses for tourists in large European cities.

How long does it take someone to walk along route:

a) A-B-C-F-D?   b) A-E-F?   c) F-C-D-E?

14 The relation "the sum of two numbers is a prime number" is applied to the set of numbers {8, 9, 10, 11, 12, 13}.

a) Represent this situation using a graph.

b) What type of connected graph is it?

15 To confirm a meeting, the members of a board of directors formed a telephone chain. The following graph illustrates this situation.

Board of directors' telephone chain

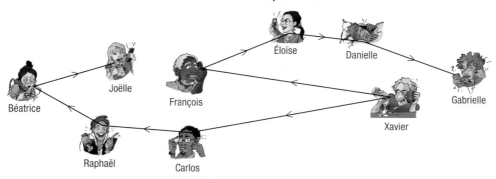

a) Based on the graph, who makes the first call?

b) What would happen if Carlos were not available to answer?

c) The person who makes the first call would like to add two calls to the telephone chain to ensure that all the members of the board of directors will be reached. Determine which two calls should be made.

16 The graph below represents the lakes at an outfitting camp and the access roads leading to those lakes. To reduce road maintenance costs, the outfitter wishes to maintain only those roads that provide direct or ondirect access to each lake.

An outfitter's roads

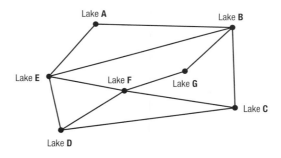

What is the maximum number of roads that can cease to be maintained?

The Province of Québec, which has over half a million lakes and some 4500 rivers, contains 3% of the planet's fresh water reserves.

17 The graph below presents a plan of the natural gas conduits that could supply various buildings in a neighbourhood.

Natural gas conduits in a neighbourhood

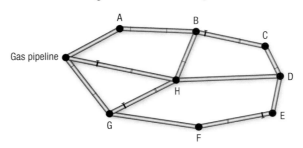

In order to save money, some of the conduits will not be installed. However, to supply all the buildings, the following conditions must be respected:

- Every conduit must be connected directly or indirectly to the gas pipeline.
- At most, three buildings can be connected to one another directly or indirectly.

Represent the modified plan using a graph.

18 **WATER CYCLE** Water makes up close to 70% of the Earth's surface and is found in different forms. Below is a representation of the water cycle.

Water cycle

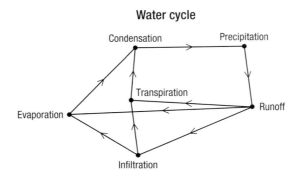

a) What does the direction of the arrows signify in this representation?

b) In your own words, explain the water cycle, starting with evaporation.

c) Identify a circuit that starts with transpiration.

d) Determine the length of:

   1) the shortest circuit that starts with evaporation

   2) the longest simple circuit that starts with evaporation

Aerial view of Niagara Falls at the border between the state of New York, United States and the province of Ontario, Canada. The falls are 52 metres high. The portion of the falls located in Canada is approximately 792 m wide.

19 Antoine, Beatrice, Caroline, Daniel and Étienne are members of the same family. Antoine is 22 years older than Étienne, Caroline is 20 years younger than Beatrice, Daniel is 3 years younger than Étienne and 5 years older than Caroline.

a) Represent this situation using a graph in which each edge expresses the relation "…is … years older than…".

b) Who is the youngest member of the family?

c) What is the age difference between:
1) Antoine and Caroline?
2) Antoine and Beatrice?

d) Considering that Caroline is 13 years old, determine the age of each family member.

20 The following graph presents cruise ship routes between the various islands of the West Indies as well as the duration (in days) of each leg.

The West Indies comprise a group of islands located in the Caribbean Sea. Many languages are spoken there, including Spanish, English and French

West Indian cruise-ship routes

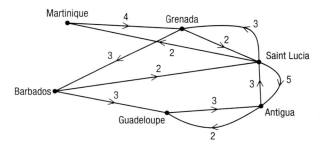

a) What is the length of a person's cruise with the following route: Saint Lucia, Martinique, Grenada and Barbados?

b) A person would like to start a cruise in Martinique, end it in Guadeloupe and visit the 6 islands without stopping at the same island twice. Determine:
1) all the possible routes
2) the duration of this route

c) A cruise ship starting in Saint Lucia and ending in Guadeloupe visits as many islands as possible once only. Which island will not be visited on this cruise?

d) A person would like to start a cruise in Saint Lucia and end it in Guadeloupe without stopping at the same island twice. Determine:
1) all the possible routes
2) the minimum duration of this cruise

21 The following graph presents the length (in km) of various routes that Louis could take as he trains for a marathon. He begins and ends each training session at his home.

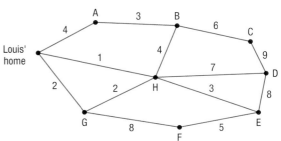

Louis' training for a marathon

a) At the beginning of his training session, Louis must run less than 10 km without taking the same road twice. Determine:

   1) the route he can take

   2) the distance travelled

b) What distance does Louis travel if he takes the following route: Home-G-F-E-H-B-A-Home?

c) Identify two routes that would allow Louis to cover between 30 and 35 km without taking the same road twice.

22 An airline offers flights to European destinations. The following graph indicates the flight time (in h) between pairs of cities.

Flight routes between various European cities

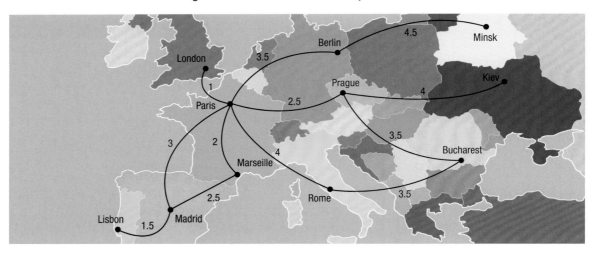

a) 1) At least how many different flights must a person take to travel from London to Minsk?

   2) How much time will this person spend in an airplane?

b) If it is 6:00 a.m. in Minsk, it is 4:00 a.m. in Lisbon. A woman leaves Minsk at 6:00 p.m. headed for Lisbon, with a one-hour stopover at each of the airports in Berlin, Paris and Madrid. Using the local time in Lisbon, determine her arrival time.

c) What is the minimum number of flight hours needed to travel from Madrid to Bucharest?

This section is related to LES 8 and 9.

PROBLEM Vehicle maintenance

Every year in Canada, over 12 billion dollars are spent on maintaining and repairing motor vehicles. This sector of the industry employs over 219 000 people who maintain or fix over 17 million vehicles.

The following tasks have to be completed in order to repair a damaged vehicle:

- PREPARING THE ESTIMATE (1 DAY)
- DELIVERY OF NEW PARTS (6 DAYS)
- REPAIRING THE VEHICLE'S REUSABLE PARTS (4 DAYS)
- PAINTING REUSABLE AND NEW PARTS (1 DAY)
- DRYING REUSABLE AND NEW PARTS (2 DAYS)
- REPAIRING THE VEHICLE'S MECHANICS (3 DAYS)
- FINAL ASSEMBLY OF THE VEHICLE (2 DAYS)
- ROAD TEST FOLLOWING REPAIRS (1 DAY)
- INSPECTION BY AN AUTHORIZED AGENT (1 DAY)
- CLEANING THE VEHICLE (1 DAY)

Explain how the mechanic can repair this vehicle in 16 days.

The travelling salesman problem has been studied in mathematics since the 19th century. Irish mathematician William Rowan Hamilton set out the problem in 1859. It consists of determining the shortest path that connects a set of cities and returning to the departure city without travelling through the same city twice.

The following graph presents the roads and cities in a region. The distance between cities is expressed in kilometres.

Marchand forain, a work created by French painter Martin Drölling in 1812.

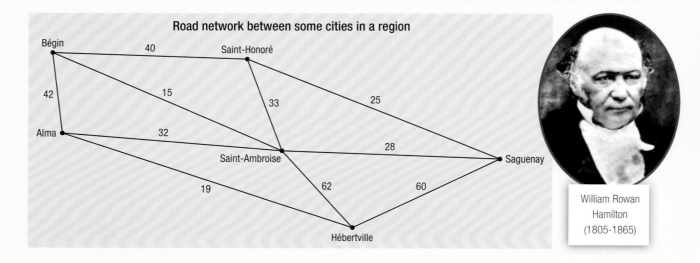

Road network between some cities in a region

William Rowan Hamilton (1805-1865)

a. 1) Identify all the different Hamiltonian circuits that begin in Saint-Ambroise.

2) Suggest a route that solves the travelling salesman problem.

Three delivery trucks leave a business in Saint-Ambroise at the same time.

b. Explain how these three trucks can deliver their merchandise to each of the other cities without returning to their starting point while minimizing the total distance travelled.

A delivery truck leaves Saint-Honoré to deliver merchandise to Hébertville.

c. What is the minimum number of roads it must take to make this delivery?

d. 1) Identify all the routes that pass through two or three different roads.

2) Of these routes:
   i) which is the shortest?   ii) which is the longest?

3) How many different roads does the shortest route contain?

4) Is the shortest route necessarily the one that represents the minimum number of different roads taken? Explain your answer.

ACTIVITY 2 Building bridges

In Québec, there are over 9000 bridges and overpasses that allow road users to travel. In 2008, approximately 650 million dollars were invested in repairing and building bridges.

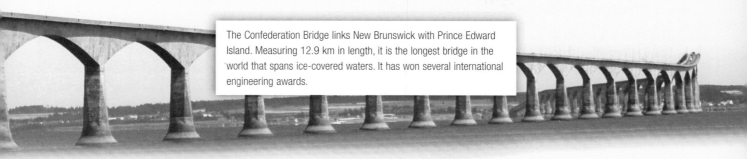

The Confederation Bridge links New Brunswick with Prince Edward Island. Measuring 12.9 km in length, it is the longest bridge in the world that spans ice-covered waters. It has won several international engineering awards.

The following table presents the main steps required to build a bridge.

Building a bridge

Step	Description	Execution time (days)	Prior steps
A	Analysis of needs	25	None
B	Development of plans	60	A
C	Manufacture of deck in a factory	35	B
D	Foundation work	45	B
E	Installation of deck	15	C and D
F	Construction of bridge approaches	20	D
G	Paving work	3	E and F
H	Verification of compliance of work	4	G
I	End of work	None	H

a. 1) Complete the graph below, which represents this situation.

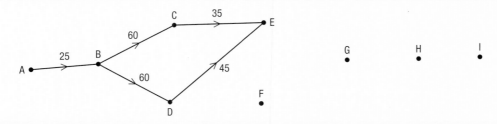

2) Why is this graph directed?

3) What do the numbers on the graph's arcs signify?

b. Based on the context, explain why paths B-C-E and B-D-E are parallel.

c. 1) Find all the paths that connect vertex A to vertex I.

2) Which path has the maximum value?

3) In this context, what does this value correspond to?

ACTIVITY 3 Producing an atlas

An atlas contains many geographical maps. In the production of an atlas, maps are generally coloured in order to properly differentiate bordering regions. Using a minimum number of colours allows production costs to be reduced.

The makers of an atlas would like to colour part of the map of France below using a minimum number of colours so that any two regions that share a border are of different colours.

The four colour theorem was first stated in 1852. It was proved in 1976 using many computer calculations.

Map of a part of France

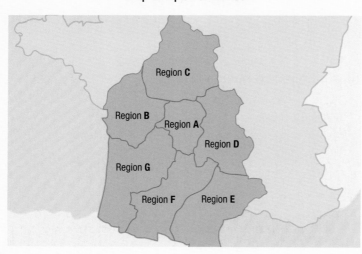

a. If Region **B** is coloured red, can red also be used for:

1) Region **A**? 　　2) Region **C**? 　　3) Region **D**?

4) Region **E**? 　　5) Region **F**? 　　6) Regions **D** and **E**?

7) Regions **D** or **E**? 　　8) Regions **D**, **E** and **F**? 　　9) Regions **D**, **E** or **F**?

In the adjacent graph, the vertices represent the regions of France, and the edges represent the cross-border lines.

Graph of a part of France

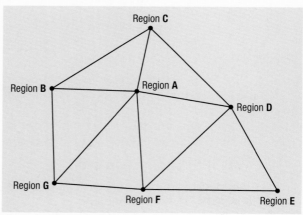

b. What is the advantage of determining the colour:

1) of the vertex of highest degree first?

2) of the vertex of lowest degree last?

c. What can be said about the colour associated with two vertices that are:

1) directly linked?

2) indirectly linked?

d. What is the minimum number of colours required to colour the map?

e. Colour the map of this part of France.

PATH OF MINIMUM VALUE

You can determine the path of minimum value connecting two vertices in a graph by indicating, at each vertex, the path of minimum value that ends at the initial vertex as well as its value.

E.g. In the graph below, the initial vertex is A and the final vertex is F.

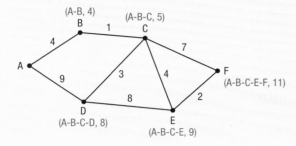

The path of minimum value is A-B-C-E-F, and its value is 11.

TREE OF MINIMUM OR MAXIMUM VALUES

You can determine a graph's tree of minimum or maximum values as follows.

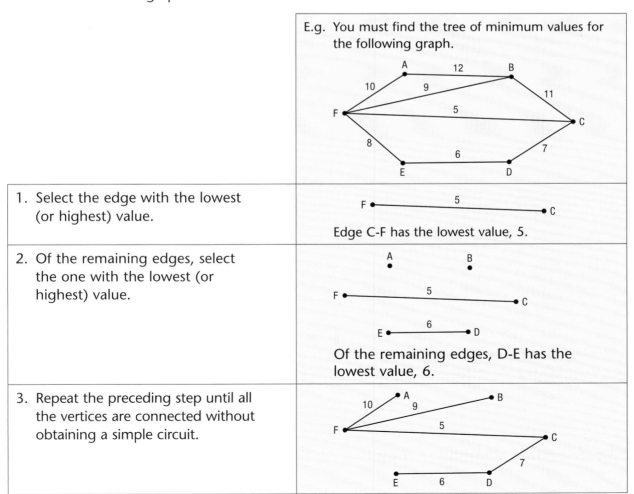

	E.g. You must find the tree of minimum values for the following graph.
1. Select the edge with the lowest (or highest) value.	Edge C-F has the lowest value, 5.
2. Of the remaining edges, select the one with the lowest (or highest) value.	Of the remaining edges, D-E has the lowest value, 6.
3. Repeat the preceding step until all the vertices are connected without obtaining a simple circuit.	

CHROMATIC NUMBER

The chromatic number is the **minimum number of colours** necessary to colour all of a graph's vertices without any two adjacent vertices being the same colour.

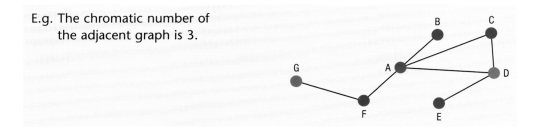

E.g. The chromatic number of the adjacent graph is 3.

It is possible to colour a graph as follows.

	E.g. You must determine the chromatic number of the following graph.
1. Colour the vertex of highest degree.	
2. Colour the vertices adjacent to the vertex of highest degree with another colour without giving two adjacent vertices the same colour.	
3. Colour the other vertices with colours that have already been used, if possible, and if not, use another colour.	

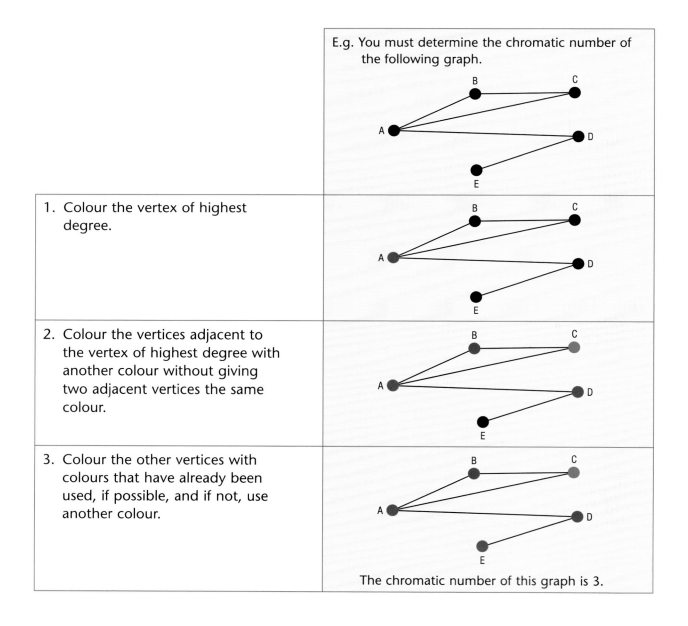

The chromatic number of this graph is 3.

CRITICAL PATH

In a graph, a critical path corresponds to a **simple path of maximum value**. Critical paths are used to determine the minimum amount of time required to carry out a task comprising several steps. To represent such a situation, you must be aware of which steps are prerequisites for others and which can be carried out simultaneously.

E.g.

Starting a company

Step	Description	Execution time (days)	Prior steps
A	Preparing a business plan	30	None
B	Conducting market research	10	A
C	Looking for partners	25	A
D	Looking for a location	20	A
E	Analyzing the market research	5	B
F	Evaluating the product-distribution system	15	C and D
G	Arranging for financing	35	E and F
H	Launching the company	None	G

The set of steps associated with starting this company can be represented using the adjacent graph. In this graph, the following can be noted:

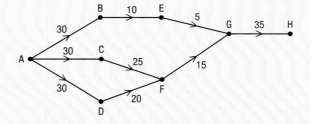

- Each vertex corresponds to a step.
- Parallel paths are associated with steps that can be executed simultaneously.
- The number indicated at each arc corresponds to the execution time of the step at the arc's starting point.

The minimum time required to start this company can be determined by finding the value of the critical path associated with this situation.

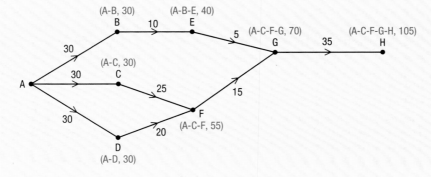

It would take a minimum of 105 days to start this company.

1 Determine the chromatic number of each of the following graphs.

a)

b)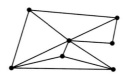

c)

d)

e)

f)

2 a) Based on the adjacent graph, represent the tree:

1) of minimum value   2) of maximum value

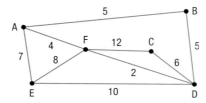

b) Are there other solutions than those found in **a)**? Explain your answer.

3 The adjacent table presents the steps involved in performing a task, the execution time and the prior steps required for each one.

a) Represent this situation using a directed, weighted graph.

b) Determine the critical path that represents this situation.

c) Determine the minimum time required to complete all the steps.

Step	Execution time (days)	Prior steps
A	1	None
B	3	A
C	2	A
D	5	A
E	4	B and C
F	1	E and D
G	None	B and F

4 Based on the adjacent graph, determine the minimum value of the path that connects:

a) vertex A to vertex D

b) vertex B to vertex E

c) vertex D to vertex F

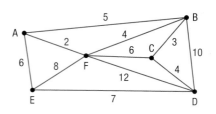

5 For each case, find:

   1) the critical path   2) the value of this path

a)
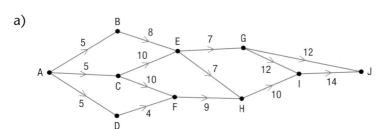

b)
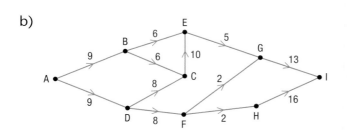

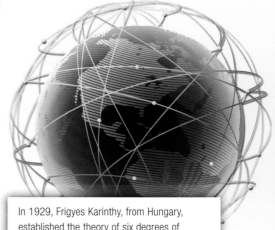

In 1929, Frigyes Karinthy, from Hungary, established the theory of six degrees of separation, which refers to the possibility that every person on the planet can be connected to any other person through a chain of acquaintances that involves five links at the most.

6 Is it possible to determine the path of greatest value that connects vertices A and D in the graph below? Explain your answer.

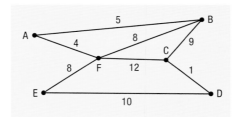

7 Below is some information about a graph with vertices D, E, F, G and H.

Edge	D-E	D-F	D-G	D-H	E-F	E-G	E-H	F-G
Value	5	8	13	9	9	15	8	10

Based on this graph, represent the tree:

a) of minimum value   b) of maximum value

8 In the adjacent graph, determine the minimum value of the path that connects vertices:

a) e and b   b) d and a

c) a and d   d) a and b

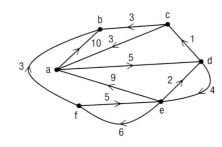

9 Based on the adjacent graph, determine:

a) 1) the Hamiltonian path of minimum value that starts at vertex E

   2) the value of this path

b) 1) the Hamiltonian path of maximum value that starts at vertex D

   2) the value of this path

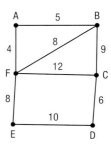

10 In the graph below, the values represent the amount (in $) that a company must pay to transport its merchandise from one city to another.

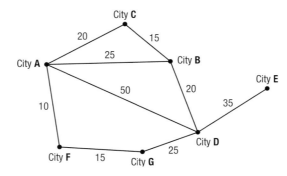

a) Determine the minimum transport cost:

   1) from City **A** to City **E**   2) from City **F** to City **B**

b) What is the minimum transport cost if a truck leaves City **E** and delivers a package to every other city?

> The transportation of goods by road is an important factor in the North American economy. In Québec, because of its competitive advantages (flexibility, speed and cost), road transport dominates all other goods' transportation methods.

11 The vertices of a graph are P, Q, R, S, T and U, and its edges are P-Q, P-R, P-U, P-S, P-T, Q-R, R-S, R-U, S-T and S-U.

a) Illustrate this graph.

b) Determine this graph's chromatic number.

12 a) Find the chromatic number for each of the trees below.

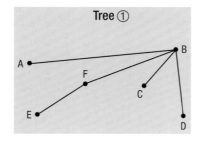

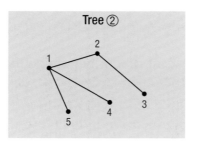

b) 1) Formulate a conjecture about a tree's chromatic number.

   2) Verify your conjecture using a tree of order 8.

13 The graph below illustrates the installation costs ($ in thousands) of power lines that connect certain cities to a wind farm.

a) If all the power lines are installed, what is the total cost of the network?

b) 1) Using a graph, represent an electrical network that meets the following criteria:

- Each city must be directly or indirectly connected to the wind farm by a power line.
- The total installation cost must be minimal.

2) Determine the minimum installation cost for this network.

Cities connected to a wind farm

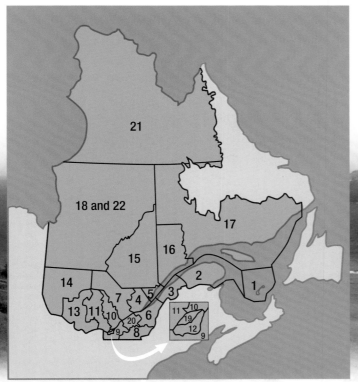

c) What is the difference between the installation cost of the original network in **a)** and the minimum installation cost of the modified network?

 14 TOURIST REGIONS Québec has 22 tourist regions that each offer different attractions.

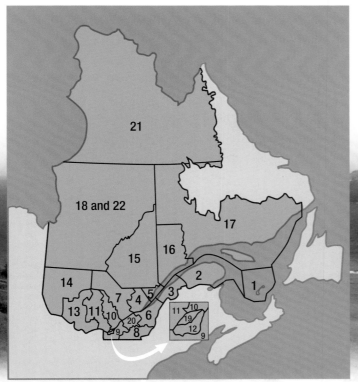

The Gaspé Peninsula, which covers 21 000 km² and juts out into the Gulf of St. Lawrence, is unique for its distinct shape, sites and contrasting landscapes. It is Québec's premier tourist region.

a) Represent Québec's touristic regions using a graph in which an edge corresponds to a shared border between two regions.

b) Determine this graph's chromatic number.

c) Colour this map using a minimum number of colours. Two touristic regions with a shared border must be of different colours.

15

A manager prepares work schedules for her nine employees. In the table below, an X signifies that the two employees cannot work simultaneously.

Work schedules

	Employee A	Employee B	Employee C	Employee D	Employee E	Employee F	Employee G	Employee H	Employee I
Employee A		X		X			X	X	
Employee B	X			X		X		X	
Employee C							X		X
Employee D	X	X							X
Employee E									
Employee F		X					X		X
Employee G	X		X			X			
Employee H	X	X							
Employee I			X	X		X			

a) Is it possible to create teams of three employees if each employee can only be a part of one work team?

b) The manager must find someone to replace her if she is absent. Which employee should she identify? Explain your answer.

16

The graph below represents a taxi ride's travel time (in min) between two intersections.

Travelling by taxi

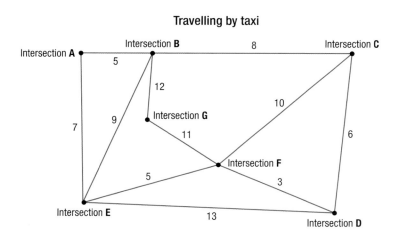

a) Calculate the minimum time to get from:
   1) Intersection **F** to Intersection **B**
   2) Intersection **A** to Intersection **D**

b) Find a Hamiltonian path of minimum value that starts at Intersection **F**.

17 An accounting firm hires a company to review its computer system. The following is the company's proposal for the implementation of a new system:

Implementation of a computer system

Step	Description	Execution time (days)	Prior steps
A	Analysis of needs	10	None
B	Detailed analysis of project	8	A
C	Purchase of computers	21	B
D	Training of programming team	3	B
E	Designing the accounting system	6	C
F	Coding of the accounting system	18	C
G	Updating of the computers	5	E and F
H	Installation and delivery of the computers and accounting system	4	D and G
I	End of computer work	None	H

a) Represent this situation using a directed, weighted graph.

b) Determine the critical path that represents this situation.

c) Is it realistic to believe that the computer system will be operational in 60 days? Explain your answer.

d) Can the project's delivery date be modified if:

   1) the design of the accounting system only required 4 days? Explain your answer.

   2) the purchase of the computers only required 13 days? Explain your answer.

18 MUNICIPAL MERGERS In 2002, many municipalities in the same region were merged. The map below identifies eight boroughs in Québec City after the merger. Colour this map using a minimum number of colours. Two boroughs that share a border must be of different colours.

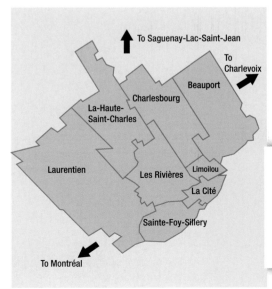

To Saguenay-Lac-Saint-Jean

To Charlevoix

Beauport

Charlesbourg

La-Haute-Saint-Charles

Laurentien

Les Rivières

Limoilou

La Cité

Sainte-Foy-Sillery

To Montréal

The main objective of Québec's municipal reorganization was to link the suburbs with the big cities, despite the opposition of certain citizens' groups. These mergers, which were made official on January 1, 2002 through the adoption of Bill 170, led to the creation of five mega-cities in the Montréal, Québec City and Outaouais regions, thus changing the mapping of these areas.

19 A young chef is having friends over for dinner. The chef starts preparing at 3:45 p.m. The steps required in the dinner's preparation are as follows.

Dinner preparation

Step	Description	Execution time (min)	Prior steps
A	Choosing the menu	5	None
B	Peeling the carrots	5	A
C	Preparing the meatballs	15	A
D	Preparing the meatball sauce	5	B
E	Cooking the meatballs in the sauce with the carrots	45	C and D
F	Preparing the salad	10	D
G	Preparing the shrimp appetizer	15	C
H	Cooking the shrimp	15	G
I	Preparing the dessert	20	G
J	Setting the table	10	E and F
K	Serving dinner	5	H, I, J
L	End of dinner preparation	None	K

a) Represent this situation using a directed, weighted graph.

b) Is it possible for dinner to be served at 5:00 p.m.? Explain your answer.

20 The following table presents the roads that connect seven historic sites as well as the distances between the sites.

a) Determine the minimum distance to be travelled from:
   1) the castle to the parliament
   2) the garden to the observatory

b) 1) Identify the shortest route that starts and ends at the castle and allows every site to be visited just once.

   2) What is the distance travelled?

Historic sites

Route		Distance (m)
Site	Site	
Castle	Wells	100
Castle	Square	220
Castle	Garden	160
Wells	Observatory	160
Square	Garden	500
Square	Parliament	300
Square	Observatory	400
Garden	Parliament	330
Prison	Parliament	200
Prison	Observatory	150
Parliament	Observatory	120

England's Windsor Castle has been continuously inhabited since the beginning of the 1000s.

21 The following table presents the steps required in the construction of a model sailboat.

Construction of a model

Step	Description	Execution time (days)	Prior steps
A	Choosing a model	2	None
B	Buying wood and glue	1	A
C	Buying the sails and the shrouds	1	A
D	Assembling the hull	14	B
E	Assembling the keel	3	B
F	Assembling the masts and sails	6	B and C
G	Buying the paint	1	D
H	Assembling the deck	5	E
I	Assembling the deckhouse and cockpit	7	E
J	Painting all the wood pieces	3	G, H and I
K	Assembling the sailboat base	1	F
L	Final assembly	3	J and K
M	End of assembly	None	L

a) What is the minimum time required to build this model?

b) Nathan assembles the hull in 8 days. He estimates that his model will be finished 6 days earlier than planned. Is he right? Explain your answer.

22 UNDERGROUND RAILROAD In the 19th century, many people from the southern United States found refuge in Canada by travelling through a network of roads called the Underground Railroad. The map below illustrates the distances (in km) between some American cities through which the refugees could travel.

a) Determine the distance between:
   1) Zanesville and Cleveland
   2) Dayton and Mansfield

b) A person travels from Dayton to Toledo through Chillicothe, Columbus and Marion at a speed of 50 km/day. How long will it take the person to reach the destination?

c) A person leaving Chillicothe would like to get to Toledo by travelling less than 350 km. What are the possible travel routes?

Road network

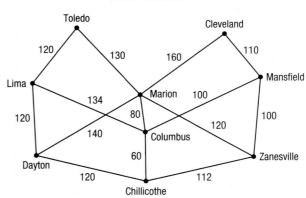

Chronicle of the past

Claude Berge

Claude Berge (1926-2002)

His life

Frenchman Claude Berge is known for his mathematical genius and his artistic talent. In 1960, he co-founded the *Oulipo* literary group and sought to demonstrate how mathematics can help create works of literature. In 1994, he published "Who killed the Duke of Densmore," a short story in which the use of graph theory allows the murderer to be identified.

Graph theory

In 1958, Claude Berge published the book *The Theory of Graphs and its Applications*. The primary goal of this work was to show that it is possible, using graphs, to visualize complex theoretical concepts. Berge is considered one of the founders of graph theory. In his works, he uses the expressions "regular graph," "planar graph" and "complement graph," and the definitions of each expression follow.

Definition	Example
Regular graph: Graph in which all vertices have the same degree.	Below is a regular graph of degree 2:
Planar graph: Graph that can be represented such that the edges only intersect at their vertices.	Graph A-C-B-E-D is planar since edge A-C can be drawn without touching edge B-E.
Complement graph: Two graphs are complements if they have the same vertices, have no edges in common and form a complete graph when their edges are combined.	Below are two complement graphs:

During the 1960s, with the help of mathematicians and chess champions, Claude Berge developed algorithms that are still used today in programming electronic chess games.

Games

Berge demonstrated that using graphs is often helpful in establishing winning strategies in games. The game of Nim is an example. The following are the rules of the game:

- There is a bag of 6 marbles and two players compete.
- Taking turns, the players remove 1 or 2 marbles from the bag.
- Whoever removes the last marble from the bag loses.

This game can be represented using the adjacent graph in which an arrow corresponds to the action of removing 1 or 2 marbles.

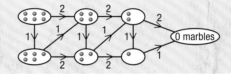

Using a graph, you can work out a winning strategy as follows.

- If there is 1 marble left, you must remove it, and you lose. Therefore, the 1-marble vertex is a "loser."
- If there are 2 or 3 marbles left, you pull out 1 or 2 marbles respectively, and your opponent, who is left with a single marble to pull out, necessarily loses. Therefore, the 2- and 3-marble vertices are "winners."
- If there are 4 marbles left, you can pull out 1 or 2 marbles, leaving 2 or 3 marbles and placing your opponent in a winning situation. Therefore, the 4-marble vertex is a "loser."
- By continuing this process, you obtain the adjacent graph.

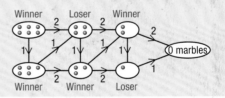

The player who starts the game can win by adopting a strategy that will result in the other player having 1 or 4 marbles to choose from at some point in the game.

1. The adjacent graph indicates the familial relationships among 5 people.

a) Is this graph regular? Explain your answer.

b) Is this graph planar? Explain your answer.

c) 1) Draw the complement of this graph.

2) Provide the meaning of the edges in the complement graph.

2. You are asked to play a game of Nim. The bag contains 8 marbles, and you must start the game. Is this an advantage? Explain your answer.

In the workplace

Performance-venue technical directors

The profession

Performance-venue technical directors manage human and material resources. They are primarily responsible for buying and maintaining lighting and sound equipment, for training stage staff and for planning the stage set-up and take-down. They must also design or interpret a show's technical specifications, which indicate the layout of lighting, sets and sound amplifiers.

Planning a show

The adjacent table presents the tasks needed to prepare *Fit of Laughter*, a comedy show.

Organizing a comedy show

	Task	Execution time (min)	Prior tasks
A	Reading the show's technical specifications	45	None
B	Preparing the lighting elements	150	A
C	Unloading equipment from the tour truck	30	B
D	Pre-assembling the set	75	C
E	Finalizing the lighting	60	C
F	Securing the lighting to the ceiling	20	E
G	Finalizing the assembly of the set	30	D and F
H	Preparing the sound system	60	F
I	Preparing floor lighting	45	G
J	Fine-tuning the lighting	45	I
K	Checking sound and lights	20	H and J
L	End of show organization	None	K

Human resource management

Often, the members of a technical team are charged with several tasks related to the preparation of a show; this complicates human resource management.

For example, nine people who are specialized in different domains are available for the preparation of the show *Sensational*. The technical director must put together a work team consisting of three people.

Adjacent is some information on the efficiency of the teamwork of these nine people.

- Beatrice's work with Danny or Francine is inefficient.
- Francine and Danny cannot work together.
- Eli does not work well with Charles, Danny, Gaston or Hector.
- The venue will not be set up fully if Danny works with Hector.
- Charles and Gaston cannot work together.
- Alexandra and Charles do not make a competent team.
- Isabelle can work with anyone.

Performance lighting

Technical directors sometimes use a graph to organize the electrical connections in a lighting system. For example, the graph below presents the different ways a lighting system can be connected to the stage's electrical box for the show *Clara*.

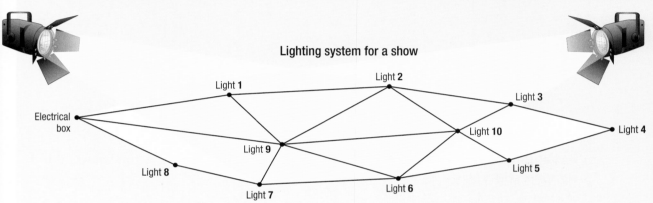

Lighting system for a show

Light **1** Light **2** Light **3** Light **4**
Electrical box Light **10** Light **9** Light **8** Light **7** Light **6** Light **5**

Lights **1**, **8** and **10** are of Type **A**, Lights **2**, **3**, **5** and **6** are of Type **B**, and Lights **4**, **7** and **9** are Type **C**. In order to avoid creating a short circuit, the following must be done:

- Every light must be directly or indirectly connected to the electrical box.
- The number of electrical connections must be kept to the minimum.
- A maximum of 2 lights of Type **A** and 2 lights of Type **B** can be connected.
- A maximum of 2 lights of Type **B** and 2 lights of Type **C** can be connected.
- A maximum of 1 light of Type **A** and 4 lights of Type **C** can be connected.

1. Calculate the minimum time required to prepare the venue for the comedy show *Fit of laughter*.

2. For the preparation of the show *Sensational*, list all the teams that the technical director can form with Eli.

3. Propose an arrangement for the lighting system for the show *Clara*.

overview

1 Refer to the adjacent graph, and answer the following:

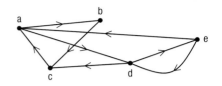

a) Is there an Euler path? If so, identify it.

b) Identify a Hamiltonian path.

c) Is there a Hamiltonian circuit? If there is, identify it.

2 a) In the graph below, find an Euler circuit.

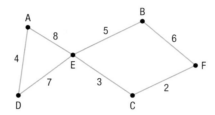

b) What is the value of this Euler circuit?

c) What do you notice in comparing the value of this Euler circuit to the values of the graph's edges?

3 For a certain project, there are 10 tasks to be completed. The table below provides information on each one:

Tasks for a project

Task	Minimum execution time (s)	Prior tasks
A	10	None
B	15	A
C	20	A
D	5	B
E	30	B and C
F	25	C
G	5	D
H	10	E and F
I	15	G
J	None	H and I

Task scheduling theory pertains to the optimal execution of tasks based on the time frames and constraints of the sequence. The use of the scheduling principle is an integral part of the realization of complex projects such as highway construction.

a) Represent this situation using a graph.

b) Find the critical path that represents this situation.

c) Determine the minimum time required to complete all the tasks.

4　a) In the adjacent graph, identify the arc that must be added in order to obtain an Euler path.

b) Identify two possible Euler paths from the graph obtained in **a)**.

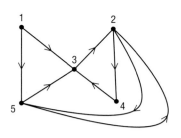

5　Represent each of the graphs described below.

a) Graph **A** is not directed.

Set of vertices: {a, b, c, d, e}

Set of edges:
{a-b, a-c, b-c, b-d, d-e, e-e}

b) Graph **B** is directed.

Set of vertices: {6, 7, 8, 9}

Set of edges:
{7-8, 9-8, 8-8, 9-9}

c) Graph **C** is not directed and weighted. Its vertices are K, L, M and N.

Graph's edge	Value of the edge
K-K	12
L-K	15
M-N	11
N-K	9
K-M	18

d) Graph **D** is directed and weighted. Its vertices are P, Q, R, S and T.

Graph's arc	Value of the arc
P-R	8
S-P	12
T-P	4
P-S	9
S-R	5

6　Below are five graphs:

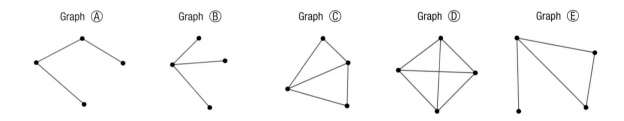

a) Complete the following table.

Graph	Ⓐ	Ⓑ	Ⓒ	Ⓓ	Ⓔ
Highest degree of its vertices					
Chromatic number					

b) Can it be stated that a graph's chromatic number is always less than $r + 1$ where r is the highest degree of its vertices? Explain your answer.

7 In the adjacent graph, identify, if possible:

a) an Euler path

b) an Euler circuit

c) a Hamiltonian path

d) a Hamiltonian circuit

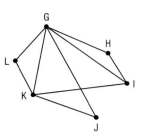

8 Determine the chromatic number of each of the following graphs.

a)
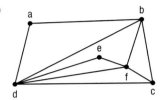

b)
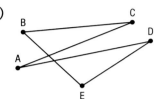

c)
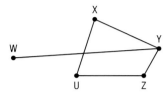

d)
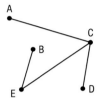

e)
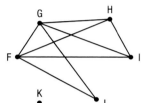

f)
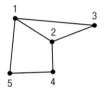

9 The graph below is weighted.

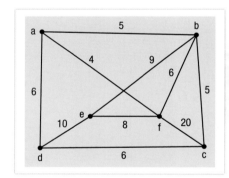

> Some scientists believe that spiderwebs could be used to develop ecosystem health indicators that gauge the presence of pollutants or chemical products to which the spiders that wove the webs were exposed.

a) Find the smallest value of the path that connects vertices:

1) a and e
2) f and c

b) Draw the tree:

1) of maximum value
2) of minimum value

c) Identify the Hamiltonian circuits of minimum value that starts at vertex c.

10 For each of the graphs below, identify an Euler circuit.

a)
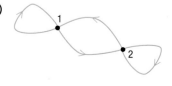

b)
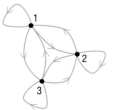

c)
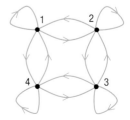

11 In the following graph, each value corresponds to a number of days.

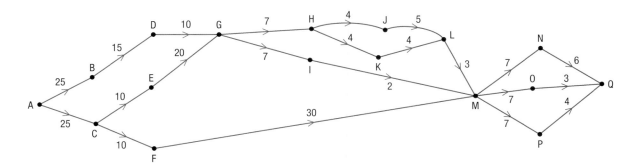

a) 1) Identify the critical path.

    2) Determine the value of the critical path.

b) If the value of arc E-G is decreased by 8, does the value of the critical path also decrease by 8 days? Explain your answer.

12 During World War II, some mathematicians assumed the planning of the allied countries' naval patrols. The graph below illustrates the routes between various ports belonging to these countries.

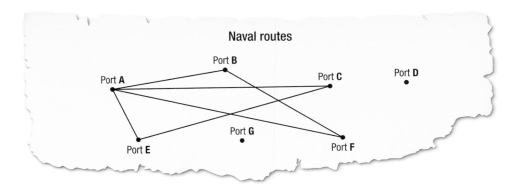

Naval routes

a) Identify the ports that do not belong to the allied countries.

b) Starting from Port **A**, is it possible to patrol all the allied ports just once?

c) Starting from Port **A**, suggest a route for an allied ship that would allow it to patrol each maritime link just once.

U-boats were German submarines used in both world wars.

13 It is possible to make words using the graph below.

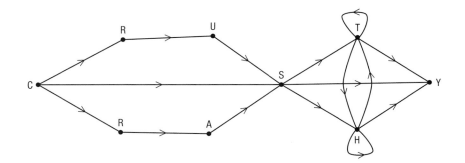

Considering that a word doesn't necessarily have any meaning, that it starts with the letter C and that it ends with the letter Y:

a) Is it possible to make the word "crastthy"? Explain your answer.

b) Is it possible to make the word "crusathy"? Explain your answer.

c) What is the shortest word that can be formed?

d) Identify all the four-letters words that can be formed.

e) Identify at least five English words that can be formed.

14 **FOREST ECOSYSTEM** There exist certain relationships between living creatures in a natural environment. In an ecosystem, insectivores feed on insects, herbivores on plants and carnivores on animal flesh. The diagram below represents a forest ecosystem.

Forest ecosystem

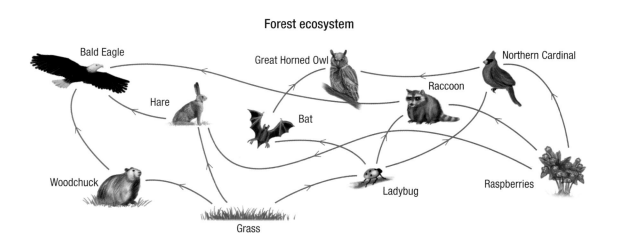

a) What is the significance of the arrows in this diagram?

b) Identify the following living creatures:
   1) the insectivores   2) the herbivores   3) the carnivores

c) What is the length of the shortest path connecting the grass to the Bald Eagle?

15 The adjacent graph shows a way of using a sewage system to connect a city's neighbourhoods to a water purification plant.

If each neighbourhood must be connected directly or indirectly to the purification plant, suggest a sewage system with a minimum number of links.

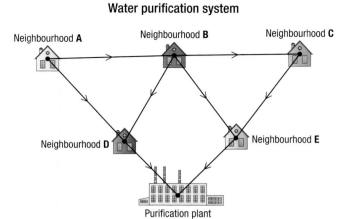

Water purification system

Neighbourhood **A**

Neighbourhood **B**

Neighbourhood **C**

Neighbourhood **D**

Neighbourhood **E**

Purification plant

16 The following are the various steps required to build a house:

Building a house

Step	Execution time (days)	Prior steps
A. Developing the plans	25	None
B. Applying for and receiving a mortgage	15	A
C. Choosing a contractor	10	A
D. Choosing and buying a lot	10	B
E. Choosing building materials	15	C
F. Choosing finishing materials	25	C
G. Preparing the foundation	7	D and E
H. Framing floors and walls	4	G
I. Plumbing (first stage)	2	G
J. Framing and finishing of roof	5	H
K. Wiring for electricity	4	H
L. Plumbing (second stage)	3	J and K
M. Finishing of interior walls	7	F, I and L
N. Finishing of exterior walls	6	M
O. Installing heating systems	3	M
P. Landscaping	4	M
Q. End of construction	None	N, O and P

a) Represent this situation using a graph.

b) Find the critical path that represents this situation.

c) Determine the minimum time required to complete all the steps.

d) 1) If choosing finishing materials is done in 20 days rather than in 25 days, will building the house take 5 fewer days? Explain your answer.

2) If choosing building materials is done in 10 days rather than in 15 days, will building the house take 5 fewer days? Explain your answer.

17 CONFEDERATION In 1867, four provinces united to form Canada. Today, there are ten provinces and three territories. The map below presents Canada as it exists today.

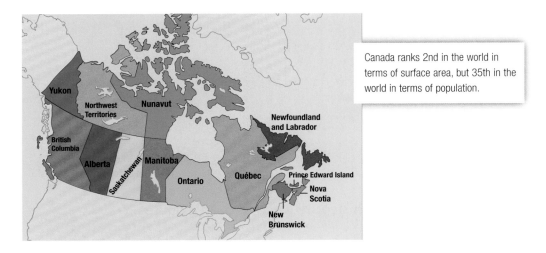

Canada ranks 2nd in the world in terms of surface area, but 35th in the world in terms of population.

Below is some information on the history of Canada:

Historic events

Year	Provinces or territories added
1867	Ontario, Québec, New Brunswick, Nova Scotia
1870	Northwest Territories, Manitoba
1871	British Columbia
1873	Prince Edward Island
1905	Alberta, Saskatchewan, Yukon
1949	Newfoundland
1999	Nunavut

If two adjacent regions cannot be given the same colour, determine the minimum number of colours needed to colour the geographical map of Canada in:

a) 1867   b) 1871   c) 1905   d) 1999

18 The edges of the graph below represent the routes that a mobile canteen can take. The values correspond to the revenue generated by taking that particular route. A canteen's route starts at Intersection **D** and crosses each intersection only once. Determine the route that generates the maximum revenue.

Routes that a mobile canteen can take

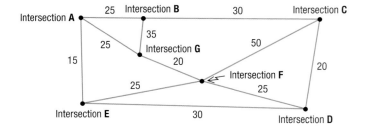

19 When a forest fire occurs, air tankers capable of dropping thousands of litres of water on the fire source are sometimes used. These planes fill up with water from lakes near the fire. The diagram below represents a region that contains several lakes and in which there occur often forest fires.

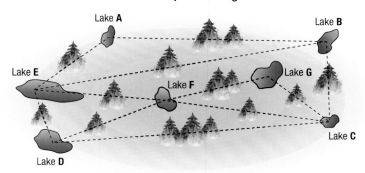

Possible routes of a plane during a forest fire

Determine the route that a plane must take in order to drop water once on each fire source.

> It takes the CL-215 approximately 10 s to scoop up 5100 L of water and store it in its reservoirs. It then drops the water on forest fires.

20 **THE TRANS CANADA TRAIL** Once it is completed, the Trans Canada Trail will be the longest recreational trail in the world. Over 21 000 km long, it will link 3 oceans, 33 million Canadians, 1000 communities and 600 local trails. The table below lists the distances between the main possible destinations.

The Trans Canada Trail

Trail		Distance (km)	Trail		Distance (km)
Victoria	Edmonton	2624	Kenora	Thunder Bay	762
Edmonton	Inuvik	3534	Thunder Bay	Hamilton	2221
Inuvik	Tuktoyaktuk	179	Hamilton	Windsor	575
Inuvik	Kakisa	1461	Hamilton	Fredericton	2267
Kakisa	Yellowknife	325	Fredericton	Halifax	790
Kakisa	Edmonton	1550	Fredericton	Charlottetown	582
Edmonton	Kenora	3271	Halifax	St. John's	1584

a) Represent the Trans Canada Trail using a weighted graph.

b) Find the shortest route that links Thunder Bay to Inuvik.

c) What is the shortest distance between St. John's and Victoria?

THE CHANNEL TUNNEL The Channel Tunnel is a 49.7-km-long rail tunnel linking Great Britain and France. It was inaugurated on May 6, 1994. Construction took place on both sides of the Channel. The following table presents the different stages of construction and their approximate duration.

Work on both shores of the tunnel under the Channel

	Stage	French side		British side	
		Execution time (months)	Prior stages	Execution time (months)	Prior stages
A	Digging an access shaft at Sangatte (Phase 1)	4	None	None	None
B	Digging an access shaft at Sangatte (Phase 2)	7	A	None	None
C	Building a manufacturing plant for the tunnel's arches	8	A	8	None
D	Manufacturing the tunnel's first arches	3	C	3	C
E	Constructing the tunnel	40	B and D	48	D
F	Preparing the terminal (Phase 1)	45	C	45	C
G	Connecting the tunnels under the Channel	3	E	3	E
H	Preparing the terminal (Phase 2)	16	E and F	10	E and F
I	Finishing work	2	G and H	2	G and H
J	End of work	None	I	None	I

a) Work began in September 1987. When did each country finish its portion of the work?

b) Identify two stages that could have sped up the work had they been completed more quickly.

In 1751, French engineer Nicolas Desmarets first suggested that a tunnel be built under the Channel to improve the means of communication between France and England. Drilling first began in 1875 but was soon abandoned for military reasons. In 1972, an agreement to build the tunnel was reached, but work was once again halted, this time for economic reasons, and the galleries became flooded. Finally, in 1987, work began in earnest, and the rail tunnel was inaugurated in 1994.

22 In the 19th century, salesmen would go from house to house to distribute ice so that people could preserve their perishable goods. The graph below illustrates the various storerooms used by an ice salesman and the distance (in km) that separates them.

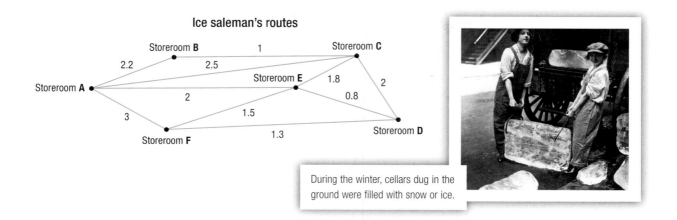

Ice saleman's routes

During the winter, cellars dug in the ground were filled with snow or ice.

The starting point is Storeroom **A**. Determine the route that allows the salesman to service every storeroom a single time while minimizing the total distance travelled.

23 Toll booths are installed on some roads to finance the road network. The graphs below provide information related to the future construction of a road network.

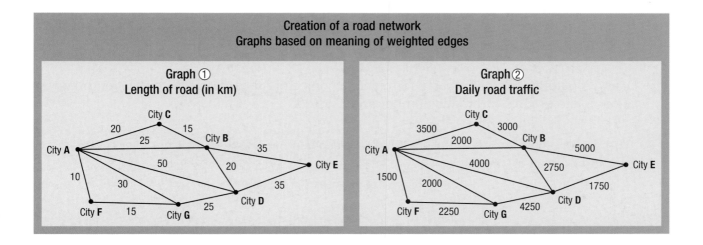

Creation of a road network
Graphs based on meaning of weighted edges

The construction cost of 1 km of road is $1.5 million, and it costs $3/vehicle to use a road between two cities in this network. Propose a simplified version of this network to the Ministry of Transport whereby each city is directly or indirectly linked to every other city and the network is as profitable as possible.

1 Ambulance drivers must quickly evaluate the shortest route to the location of an emergency call. The graph below illustrates the possible routes between various locations. The values represent the distances (in m) between two locations.

An ambulance's routes between its starting point and the hospital

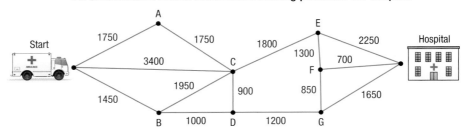

Below is some information regarding an intervention:

- The ambulance travels at a mean speed of 70 km/h.
- 2 min elapse between the emergency call and the ambulance's departure.
- 7 min elapse between the ambulance's arrival on the scene of the accident and its departure for the hospital.
- 3 min elapse between the time the person leaves the ambulance and the time that this person is taken care of by hospital staff.

An ambulance must travel to point C to rescue a patient and bring him or her to the hospital. Determine the minimum time elapsed until that person is taken care of by hospital staff.

2 Using a mathematical approach, formulate a conjecture regarding the connection between a complete graph's chromatic number and its order.

3 The graph below shows the routes that a salesperson can take to visit her clients. The starting point is located at point A.

Routes that a salesperson can take

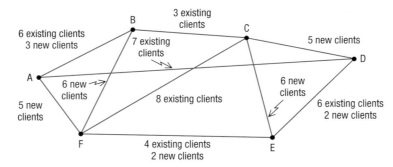

A visit to an existing client brings in $20, and a visit to a new client brings in $25. Suggest a route that allows the salesperson to maximize profits, travel along at most 6 roads, never along the same road twice and return to the starting point.

4 The map of a region's cities is represented using a graph of order 7 in which the vertices correspond to the cities and the edges represent the relation "… has at least one shared border with …." The degrees of the vertices are 6, 5, 4, 4, 3, 2 and 2. Create a possible representation of a map of this region using a minimum number of colours such that no two adjacent cities are the same colour.

5 Below is a schedule of tasks related to graduation activities at a high school:

Planning of graduation activities

	Step	Execution time (days)
A	Formation of the organizing committee	8
B	Survey of students' preferences	10
C	Choice of ring supplier	8
D	Choice of yearbook printer	10
E	Choice of photographer	9
F	Choice of venue for graduation dance	15
G	"Bake-sale" fundraiser	25
H	"Citrus-fruit-sale" fundraiser	22
I	Graduate pictures	3
J	Writing of yearbook	35
K	Layout and delivery of yearbook	40
L	Decoration of venue	2
M	End of planning	None

The following restrictions apply to these tasks:

• The pictures must be taken after the "Bake-sale" fundraiser.

• The yearbook layout must be done after the "Citrus-fruit-sale" fundraiser.

• The two fundraisers cannot take place at the same time.

• Steps **C** through **F** must be completed before steps **G** through **M** are carried out.

Suggest a schedule of tasks that allows all the steps to be completed in less than 150 days.

6 A zoologist must put incompatible animal breeds in different enclosures. The adjacent table presents the incompatibilities among certain breeds.

Incompatible animal breeds

Breed incompatible with Breed **B**	A
Breeds incompatible with Breed **E**	A, D, F, G, H
Breeds incompatible with Breed **F**	A, C, D, E, G, H
Breeds incompatible with Breed **G**	A, C, D, E, F

The manufacturing cost C of an enclosure (in $) is given by the rule
$C = 500r^2 + 2000$ where r is the number of animal breeds in an enclosure.

Determine the minimum cost of separating all these breeds of animals so that no animal is in danger.

7 Using a milling machine saves time and energy when drilling holes repeatedly. A numerically controlled milling machine uses a system of coordinates.

A Cartesian plane, scaled in metres, has been superimposed onto a sheet of metal. The holes to be drilled are identified with letters. The milling machine, which moves at a speed of 1.5 m/s and drills a hole in 10 s, starts and ends its course at the origin of the Cartesian plane. For each movement, the milling machine can cover a maximum distance of 10 m. What is the least amount of time it takes the milling machine to drill the five holes and return to its starting point?

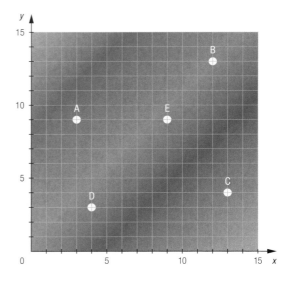

Milling is a machining process involving the removal of chips of material. The tool used, called a milling machine, allows all types of shapes to be reproduced, even complex ones. This tool can be used on many materials: wood, plaster, resin, plastic, aluminum. The digital milling machine, which is controlled by computer, is a state-of-the-art machining tool.

8 **RALLY** The Rallye Aïcha des Gazelles is a challenge held in the Sahara Desert wherein teams of two compete in a rally using a map and a compass. The goal of the rally is to find checkpoints while travelling as few kilometres as possible.

Below is some information about six people who would like to sign up for the rally.

- Alexandra cannot work with Éloïse, Frédérique or Genevieve.
- Beatrice cannot be teamed up with Danielle or Éloïse.
- Genevieve and Frédérique are not a good combination.

The map below illustrates one of the stages of the race.

Possible routes for a stage in the rally

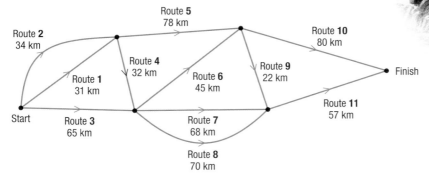

The Rallye Aïcha des Gazelles is an adventure sport competition for women only; it takes place in the Moroccan desert. All types of motorized land vehicles are permitted: 4 by 4, motorcycle, ATV, dune buggy, prototype, etc. The winners are those who travel the fewest kilometres, reach the most checkpoints and require the least breakdown assistance.

Suggest possible teams for the competitors, and find the shortest route for this stage.

9 A planar graph is a graph in which the edges only intersect at their vertices. The adjacent illustration represents the cavalier perspective of a regular hexagonal-based prism.

Represent this prism using a weighted planar graph.

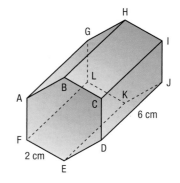

10 The vertices in the graph below represent countries of the world where it is possible to organize a car race. The values of the edges represent the total cost of transporting the cars from one place to another.

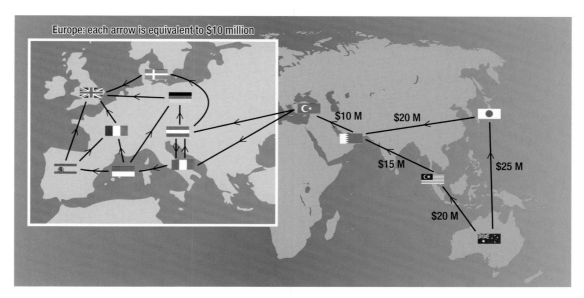

The table below presents the potential revenue for each country where a race could be held.

Potential revenue

Country		Revenue ($ in millions)	Country		Revenue ($ in millions)
Australia		80	Monaco		100
Malaysia		70	Spain		70
Japan		75	France		60
Bahrain		85	Germany		65
Turkey		75	Denmark		75
Hungary		65	Great Britain		80
Italy		90			

Car racing generates millions of dollars in economic activity throughout the world. Formula 1 races receive the most media coverage.

An organization wants to hold eight races, with the first taking place in Australia and the last in Great Britain. To obtain the maximum profit, it selects the eight locations that generate the highest revenue.

Verify whether this selection is the most profitable. If it isn't, suggest a more efficient alternative.

VISI4N

Probability and voting procedures

Is it possible to predict or even control random events? Can the result of a vote reflect the entire set of individual preferences? Can the voting procedure used to count the votes during an election affect the result? In "Vision 4," you will use new probability tools and calculate the probability that an event will occur given that another event has already occurred. You will familiarize yourself with various voting procedures. In addition to discovering the advantages and disadvantages of each of these procedures, you will learn to analyze the results of a vote or an election.

Arithmetic and algebra

Geometry

Graphs

Probability

- Mutually exclusive, non-mutually exclusive, independent and dependent events
- Conditional probability
- Comparing and interpreting different voting procedures

LEARNING AND
EVALUATION
SITUATIONS   Democracy

Chronicle of the
past   Nicolas de Condorcet

In the
workplace   Politicians

PRIOR LEARNING **1** Transmitting a radio signal

The diagram below illustrates a transmitter, a receiver and three relays, which allow a radio signal to be transmitted. The probability of a power outage at Relay ① is 10%, that at Relay ② is 4% and that at Relay ③ is 13%.

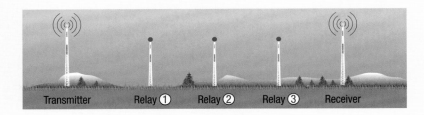

a. Complete the probability tree below.

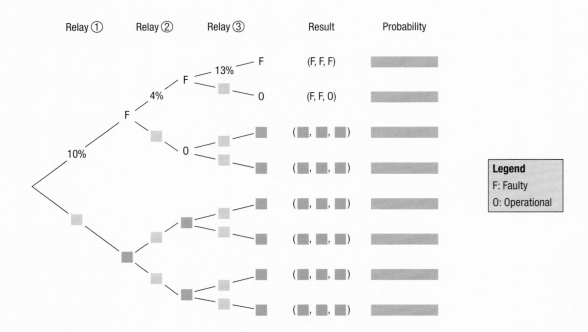

Legend
F: Faulty
O: Operational

b. What is the probability that:
1) Relays ① and ② are faulty?
2) the three relays are faulty?
3) at most two relays are faulty?
4) all the relays are operational?

The following tables provides information regarding three municipal schools.

Distribution of students

School	A	B	C
Number of students	1450	723	987

Family income

School A		School B		School C	
Family income ($ in thousands)	Percentage of students	Family income ($ in thousands)	Percentage of students	Family income ($ in thousands)	Percentage of students
[20, 30[	10	[20, 30[	2	[20, 30[	0
[30, 40[	7	[30, 40[	23	[30, 40[	6
[40, 50[	22	[40, 50[	42	[40, 50[	5
[50, 60[	24	[50, 60[	11	[50, 60[	12
[60, 70[	25	[60, 70[	13	[60, 70[	19
[70, 80[	6	[70, 80[	5	[70, 80[	32
[80, 90[	4	[80, 90[	3	[80, 90[	17
[90, 100[	2	[90, 100[	1	[90, 100[	9

a. What is the mean family income for students who attend:

1) School **A**?　　　　2) School **B**?　　　　3) School **C**?

b. Which school has the highest ratio of students whose family income is $[20,000, 40,000[to students whose family income is $[80,000, 100,000[?

c. A budget of $1,000,000 is divided proportionately among these schools based on the number of students in each school. How much is allocated to:

1) School **A**?　　　　2) School **B**?　　　　3) School **C**?

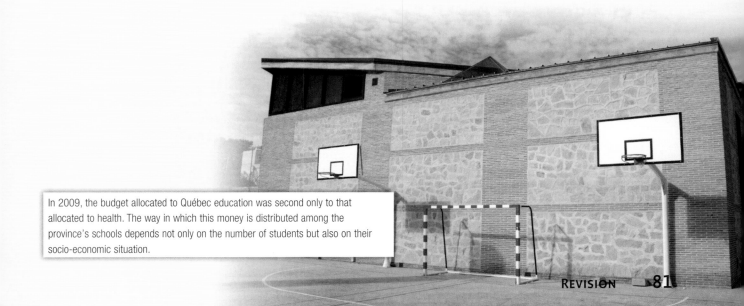

In 2009, the budget allocated to Québec education was second only to that allocated to health. The way in which this money is distributed among the province's schools depends not only on the number of students but also on their socio-economic situation.

RANDOM EXPERIMENT

An experiment is **random** if the following is true:

1. Its outcome depends on **chance**, meaning that the outcome of the experiment cannot be predicted with absolute certainty.

2. The set of all possible outcomes, called the **sample space**, can be listed before the experiment; this set is denoted by "Ω" otherwise known as "omega."

> E.g. When a six-sided die whose faces are numbered from 1 to 6 is rolled, the sample space is $\Omega = \{1, 2, 3, 4, 5, 6\}$.

EVENT

An **event** is a **subset** of the sample space. An event is considered **simple** if it consists of only **one outcome** from the sample space.

> E.g. 1) When drawing from a deck of 52 cards, "choosing a queen" is an event that corresponds to {queen of hearts, queen of spades, queen of diamonds, queen of clubs}.
>
> 2) When a coin is tossed, "landing on tails" is a simple event since it represents only one outcome {tails} of the sample space.

PROBABILITY OF AN EVENT

The **probability of an event** composed of several simple events is equal to the **sum of the probabilities** of each simple event.

> E.g. A drawer contains 8 knives, 10 forks and 12 spoons. Since "taking out a knife at random" and "taking out a fork at random" are two simple events, the probability of the event "taking out a knife or fork at random" is written as follows:
>
> $$P(\text{knife or fork}) = P(\text{knife}) + P(\text{fork}) = \frac{8}{30} + \frac{10}{30} = \frac{18}{30} = \frac{3}{5}$$

RANDOM EXPERIMENT WITH SEVERAL STEPS

By including a probability on each branch of a tree diagram, you get a **probability tree**. In a random experiment with several steps, the probability of a simple event is equal to the **product of the probabilities** of all the intermediate steps that define this event.

E.g. A marble is drawn from a bag containing 5 red marbles, 4 green marbles and 2 blue marbles. The marble is then placed back in the bag, and another is selected.

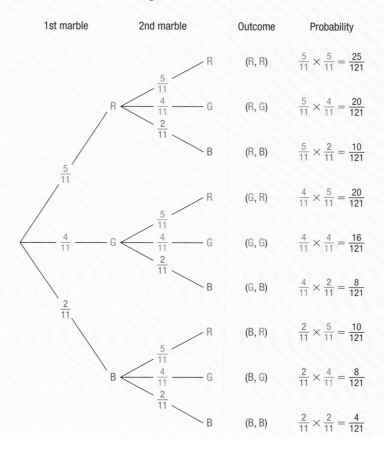

1st marble	2nd marble	Outcome	Probability
	R	(R, R)	$\frac{5}{11} \times \frac{5}{11} = \frac{25}{121}$
R	G	(R, G)	$\frac{5}{11} \times \frac{4}{11} = \frac{20}{121}$
	B	(R, B)	$\frac{5}{11} \times \frac{2}{11} = \frac{10}{121}$
	R	(G, R)	$\frac{4}{11} \times \frac{5}{11} = \frac{20}{121}$
G	G	(G, G)	$\frac{4}{11} \times \frac{4}{11} = \frac{16}{121}$
	B	(G, B)	$\frac{4}{11} \times \frac{2}{11} = \frac{8}{121}$
	R	(B, R)	$\frac{2}{11} \times \frac{5}{11} = \frac{10}{121}$
B	G	(B, G)	$\frac{2}{11} \times \frac{4}{11} = \frac{8}{121}$
	B	(B, B)	$\frac{2}{11} \times \frac{2}{11} = \frac{4}{121}$

WEIGHTED MEAN

The mean of a set of values that have varying levels of importance is called **weighted mean**.

E.g. A geography exam contains three parts. When a student's grade on each part and the relative importance of each part are taken into account, you get:

Global result = 0.75 × 0.2 + 0.72 × 0.3 + 0.88 × 0.5
            = 80.6%

Geography exam

Part	Grade (%)	Weight (%)
A	75	20
B	72	30
C	88	50

1 A box contains 26 tokens on which each of the 26 letters of the alphabet have been written. Three tokens are successively chosen at random and put back into the box. Calculate the probability of drawing:

a) three vowels

b) three consonants

c) a consonant followed by a vowel followed by a consonant

d) the letter F followed by a vowel followed by another vowel

e) the letter A followed by the letter B followed by the letter C

2 During a water quality test conducted on a river, a technician analyzes three water samples in succession to determine if they contain potable water or contaminated water. The probability of a sample being contaminated is 34%. Following are two events related to this situation:

A: only one sample is contaminated.

B: at least two samples are contamined.

a) Construct the probability tree associated with this situation.

b) Enumerate the results comprising event **A**.

c) Calculate the probability of event **B**.

d) Describe a simple event associated with this situation.

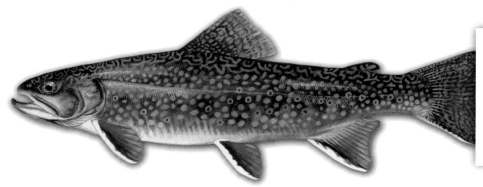

The brook trout requires a very clean aquatic environment in which to live. It needs clear, fresh and well-oxygenated waters. This species of fish is extremely sensitive to pollution. It is therefore an excellent indicator of the quality of its ecosystem.

3 A jar contains 5 red marbles, 3 yellow marbles and 2 black marbles. Three marbles are drawn consecutively. Calculate the probability of selecting the following:

a) one marble of each colour if the marbles are replaced after each selection

b) two red marbles and one black marble if they are not replaced

c) three marbles of the same colour if they are not replaced

d) two black marbles and one yellow marbles if they are replaced

4 Maëva pays $3 and spins the wheel shown in the adjacent diagram. Determine the probability that she:

a) loses all her money on the first spin

b) wins $4 on the first spin

c) wins $10 on the second spin

d) spins the wheel 4 times

5 Naomi's French grades over the course of the first term are as follows:

> Essay: 75%
>
> Reading comprehension: 82%
>
> Oral presentation: 79%

Determine Naomi's grade for the term given that the following is true:

- The essay portion is worth 40% of the term's grade.
- The reading comprehension portion is worth 45% of the term's grade.
- The oral presentation portion is worth 15% of the term's grade.

6 In a country, passenger vehicle licence plates are composed of three digits followed by three letters. Digits and letters may be repeated. If a licence plate is chosen at random, what is the probability that:

a) the first number is 7?

b) the two first letters are ZZ?

c) the three letters spell the word "FIN"?

d) the three digits make up the number 123?

The motto *Je me souviens* dates back to the 1880s. The Deputy Minister of Québec's Department of Crown Lands, Eugène-Étienne Taché, decided to inscribe it above the main entrance to the Parliament Building, which he designed. It became Québec's official motto in 1939.

7 A coin is tossed 4 times consecutively, and the side facing upward is noted each time.

a) Construct a probability tree that represents this situation.

b) What is the probability of obtaining 4 identical outcomes?

c) What is the probability of obtaining tails 2 times and heads 2 times?

> The first coin ever made in Canada, in 1908, was the 50-cent coin, which bore the effigy of Edward VII, King of the United Kingdom and the countries of the Commonwealth in the early 1900s.

8 A bag contains 4 quarters and 5 loonies. A person randomly draws 2 coins consecutively from this bag. For each case, determine the probability of the event if the person:

1) does not put the first coin back in the bag

2) puts the first coin back in the bag

a) *P*(selecting coins with a total value of $0.50)

b) *P*(selecting coins with a total value of $1.25)

c) *P*(selecting coins with a total value of $2.00)

9 Anti-spam software is designed to identify unwanted emails. Amie installs one of these programs on her computer. She estimates:

- a probability of 15% that the program will identify an email as unwanted when it is not

- a probability of 88% that the program will identify an email as unwanted when it is

- a probability of 12% that the program will identify an email as acceptable when it is not

- a probability of 85% that the program will identify an email as acceptable when it is

Amie receives an unwanted email followed by two acceptable emails. What is the probability that the program:

a) handled all emails correctly?

b) handled all emails incorrectly?

c) handled at least one email incorrectly?

> The term "spam" generally refers to unwanted email. The first spam message was sent in 1978 to approximately 600 users of the ARPANET network, a predecessor to the Internet.

10 A 6-sided die whose faces are numbered 1 to 6 is rolled 5 times, and the following results are obtained: 2, 2, 4, 6 and 2. Following this experiment, three people make predictions regarding the result of the next roll.

I THINK THE PROBABILITY OF OBTAINING AN EVEN NUMBER IS GREATER THAN THAT OF OBTAINING AN ODD NUMBER.

WELL, I THINK THAT THE PROBABILITY OF OBTAINING AN ODD NUMBER IS GREATER THAN THAT OF OBTAINING AN EVEN NUMBER.

IT LOOKS LIKE THE PROBABILITY OF OBTAINING AN EVEN NUMBER IS EQUAL TO THAT OF OBTAINING AN ODD NUMBER.

Which of these three people is right? Explain your answer.

11 The gene associated with eye colour is made up of two alleles. When a child is conceived, each parent passes on one allele. The allele that leads to brown eyes is represented by the letter B and the allele that leads to blue eyes by the letter b. Chance determines which allele is passed on by each parent.

A man and a woman, each having both B and b alleles, have a child. There is:

- a probability of 45% that the father will pass on his B allele
- a probability of 55% that the father will pass on his b allele
- a probability of 40% that the mother will pass on her B allele
- a probability of 60% that the mother will pass on her b allele

a) What is the probability that this couple's child will receive:

1) two B alleles?

2) two b alleles?

3) a B allele and a b allele?

b) Considering that the presence of two b alleles is needed for the child to have blue eyes and that the presence of a single B allele suffices for the child to have brown eyes, calculate the probability that the couple's child will have eyes that are:

1) blue

2) brown

The mechanisms that govern the hereditary transmission of certain genes were discovered by the Austrian botanist and priest Gregor Mendel, following his experiments on pea plants. The laws relating to inheritance were named *Mendel's Laws* in his honour.

This section is related to LES 10.

PROBLEM The carnival

A visitor to a carnival can participate in several games:

YOU MUST DRAW TWO MARBLES, ONE AFTER THE OTHER, FROM A BAG THAT CONTAINS 10 BLACK MARBLES AND 10 WHITE MARBLES. AFTER THE FIRST SELECTION, PUT THE MARBLE BACK IN THE BAG AND THEN DRAW ANOTHER. IF YOU GET TWO MARBLES OF DIFFERENT COLOURS, YOU WIN.

YOU MUST DRAW TWO MARBLES, ONE AFTER THE OTHER AND WITHOUT REPLACEMENT, FROM A BAG THAT CONTAINS 10 BLACK MARBLES AND 10 WHITE MARBLES. IF YOU GET TWO MARBLES OF DIFFERENT COLOURS, YOU WIN.

YOU MUST DRAW TWO MARBLES, ONE AFTER THE OTHER, FROM A BAG THAT CONTAINS 10 BLACK MARBLES AND 10 WHITE MARBLES. AFTER THE FIRST SELECTION, PUT THE MARBLE BACK IN THE BAG AND ADD A MARBLE OF THE SAME COLOUR AS THE ONE SELECTED; THEN YOU DRAW ANOTHER MARBLE. IF YOU GET TWO MARBLES OF DIFFERENT COLOURS, YOU WIN.

YOU MUST DRAW TWO MARBLES, ONE AFTER THE OTHER, FROM A BAG THAT CONTAINS 10 BLACK MARBLES AND 10 WHITE MARBLES. AFTER THE FIRST SELECTION, PUT THE MARBLE BACK IN THE BAG AND ADD A MARBLE OF THE COLOUR OTHER THAN THE ONE SELECTED; THEN YOU DRAW ANOTHER MARBLE. IF YOU GET TWO MARBLES OF THE SAME COLOUR, YOU WIN.

YOU MUST DRAW TWO MARBLES, ONE AFTER THE OTHER, FROM A BAG THAT CONTAINS 10 BLACK MARBLES AND 10 WHITE MARBLES. AFTER THE FIRST SELECTION, PUT THE MARBLE BACK IN THE BAG AND ADD A GREEN ONE; THEN YOU DRAW ANOTHER MARBLE. IF YOU GET TWO MARBLES OF DIFFERENT COLOURS, YOU WIN.

Which game should this person play to maximize the chances of winning?

Originally, one of the purposes of carnivals was to spread the latest news throughout a region. This was in addition to providing entertainment such as rides, games of skill and games of chance.

ACTIVITY 1 Medical probabilities

The results of a disease-screening test conducted on 1000 individuals are analyzed. The first medical team verifies whether each test is positive or negative. The second team verifies whether each test is valid or invalid. The following are 4 possible events and 2 Venn diagrams related to these events.

A: the test is positive.
B: the test is negative.
C: the test is valid.
D: the test is invalid.

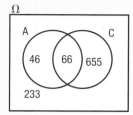

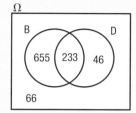

a. How many tests are:

1) positive?

2) invalid?

3) positive and valid?

4) negative or invalid?

5) positive and invalid?

6) valid or invalid?

b. Complete the two Venn diagrams below.

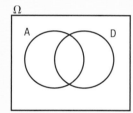

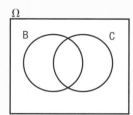

c. Two consecutive tests are chosen at random from the 1000 tests that were conducted. What is the probability of obtaining:

1) two positive tests if the first test selected is put back in with the other tests?

2) two invalid tests if the first test selected is not put back in with the other tests?

3) a valid positive test followed by an invalid negative test if the first test selected is put back in with the other tests?

4) a valid positive test followed by an invalid negative test if the first test selected is not put back in with the other tests?

A result that is said to be positive when it is not is called a "false positive."

LOGICAL CONNECTORS

The logical connectors "and" and "or" can be used to describe an event.

> E.g. A 6-sided die whose faces are numbered from 1 to 6 is rolled.
>
> - The outcome that corresponds to the event "obtaining a number that is even **and** prime" is 2 since it satisfies both characteristics stated simultaneously.
>
> - The outcomes that correspond to the event "obtaining a number that is even **or** prime" are 2, 3, 4, 5 and 6 since each one satisfies one, the other or both of the characteristics stated.

VENN DIAGRAMS

A Venn diagram allows you to graphically represent relationships among sets. In probability, each set generally corresponds to the outcomes that satisfy a given event.

In a Venn diagram, the following can be noted:

> E.g. A 10-sided die whose faces are numbered from 1 to 10 is rolled. Below are two possible events:
>
> Event A: obtaining a number greater than 5
> Event B: obtaining an even number

- The intersection of two sets A and B, written A ∩ B, is composed of elements that are common to both sets.

1)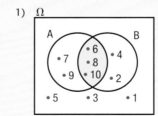

A ∩ B = {6, 8, 10}, which corresponds to numbers that are both greater than 5 **and** even.

> The symbol ∩ is often associated with the logical connector "and."

- The union of two sets A and B, written A ∪ B, is composed of all the elements in both sets.

2)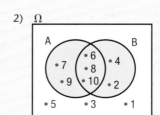

A ∪ B = {2, 4, 6, 7, 8, 9, 10}, which corresponds to numbers that are greater than 5 **or** even.

> The symbol ∪ is often associated with the logical connector "or."

MUTUALLY EXCLUSIVE EVENTS AND NON-MUTUALLY EXCLUSIVE EVENTS

Two events are mutually exclusive if they cannot occur at the same time, meaning if $A \cap B = \varnothing$.

Two events are non-mutually exclusive if they can occur at the same time, meaning if $A \cap B \neq \varnothing$.

E.g. A 6-sided die whose faces are numbered from 1 to 6 is rolled. Event A, "obtaining a number less than 3," and event B, "obtaining a number greater than 4," are mutually exclusive since $A \cap B = \varnothing$.

E.g. A 6-sided die whose faces are numbered from 1 to 6 is rolled. Event C, "obtaining an even number," and event D, "obtaining a factor of 6," are non-mutually exclusive since $C \cap D \neq \varnothing$.

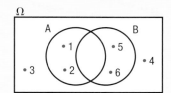

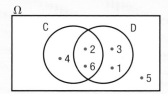

The probability of the event "obtaining a number less than 3 or a number greater than 4" is noted as follows:

$$P(A \cup B) = P(A) + P(B)$$
$$= \frac{2}{6} + \frac{2}{6}$$
$$= \frac{2}{3}$$

The probability of the event "obtaining an even number or a factor of 6" is noted as follows:

$$P(C \cup D) = P(C) + P(D) - P(C \cap D)$$
$$= \frac{3}{6} + \frac{4}{6} - \frac{2}{6}$$
$$= \frac{5}{6}$$

> You must subtract the probability of the intersection so that it is not counted twice.

Two mutually exclusive events whose union forms the set of all possible outcomes are complementary. The event that is complementary to event A is written A' and the following equation is obtained:

$$P(A) + P(A') = 1$$

INDEPENDENT EVENTS AND DEPENDENT EVENTS

Two events A and B are independent if the occurrence of one does not influence the probability of the occurrence of the other.

Two events A and B are dependent if the occurrence of one influences the probability of the occurrence of the other.

E.g. A 6-sided die numbered from 1 to 6 is rolled twice. The probability that event A, "obtaining 4 on the first roll" and event B, "obtaining 3 on the second roll" will occur is noted as follows:

$$P(A \cap B) = \frac{1}{6} \times \frac{1}{6}$$
$$= \frac{1}{36}$$

E.g. Two marbles are drawn, without replacement, from a jar containing 49 marbles numbered 1 to 49. The probability that event C, "obtaining marble 7 on the first draw" and event D, "obtaining marble 5 on the second draw" will occur is noted as follows:

$$P(C \cap D) = \frac{1}{49} \times \frac{1}{48}$$
$$= \frac{1}{2352}$$

> Since the 1st marble chosen is not put back in the vase

practice 4.1

1 For each case, determine whether events A and B are mutually exclusive. Explain your answer.

a) $P(A \cup B) = 0.75$, $P(A) = 0.45$, and $P(B) = 0.3$.

b) $P(A \cap B) = 0.1$

c) Events A and B are complementary.

d) $A \cap B = \varnothing$

2 A 6-sided die with faces numbered from 1 to 6 is rolled, and the side facing up is noted. The following are 3 possible events:

> A: obtaining an even number   B: obtaining a 3   C: obtaining a 1 or a 6

a) Can it be said that:
1) events A and B are mutually exclusive? Explain your answer.
2) events A and C are mutually exclusive? Explain your answer.

b) Calculate:
1) $P(A \cup B)$ 2) $P(A \cup C)$

Although the origin of dice is not known for certain, it is known that their first appearance dates back to prehistory.

3 Random experiments with several steps are carried out. For each case, determine whether events A and B are dependent or independent.

a) A: drawing a green marble from a bag of marbles
B: landing on heads when tossing a coin

b) A: taking a kiwi at random from a bowl of fruit and eating it
B: taking a second kiwi at random from the same bowl

c) A: obtaining a 4 when rolling a die
B: obtaining a 4 when rolling the same die a second time

The kiwi originated in China but is mainly grown in New Zealand, Italy and France. Its name stems from the resemblance between its skin and that of the bird of the same name, which is the symbol of New Zealand.

4 In a company, 45 of the 95 employees are women. Among the employees, 24 women and 32 men have a university diploma.

a) Complete a Venn diagram similar to the one shown in the adjacent illustration to represent this situation.

b) If a person is chosen at random from these employees, calculate the probability that this person is a woman or has a university diploma.

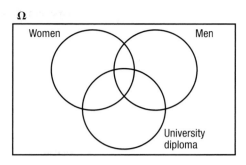

5 A person walking on the street is chosen at random, and some of that person's characteristics are recorded. For each case, determine whether events A and B are mutually exclusive or non-mutually exclusive.

a) A: the person is a man.
B: the person is a woman.

b) A: the person has blue eyes.
B: the person has brown hair.

c) A: the person's height is greater than 1.5 m.
B: the person's height is greater than 1.7 m.

d) A: the person was born in June.
B: the person was born in the summer.

Eye colour comes from melanin, which also determines hair and skin colour. The less melanin there is in the iris, the lighter the eye colour will be and vice versa.

6 Determine whether the following equalities are true or false. If the equality is false, rewrite the right side to make it true.

a) $(A \cup B) \cup C = A \cup (B \cup C)$

b) $(A \cap B) \cap C = A \cap (B \cap C)$

c) $(A \cap B) \cup C = A \cap (B \cup C)$

d) $A \cap (B \cup C) = (A \cap B) \cup (A \cap C)$

e) $A \cup (B \cap C) = (A \cup B) \cap (A \cup C)$

f) $(A \cup B)' = A' \cup B'$

g) $A \cap \varnothing = A$

h) $A \cup \varnothing = \varnothing$

7 For each case, shade the area associated with the expression provided using a Venn diagram similar to the one shown in the adjacent illustration.

a) $A \cap B$

b) $A \cup C$

c) $A \cap B \cap C$

d) $(A \cap B) \cup C$

e) $A \cap (B \cup C)$

f) $A \cup (B \cap C)$

g) $A' \cap B'$

h) $A' \cap A$

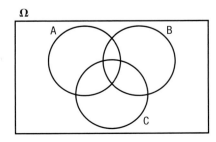

8 Using a Venn diagram, show that:

a) (A ∪ B)' = A' ∩ B'

b) (A ∩ B)' = A' ∪ B'

9 In a group of 35 people:

- 7 people are left-handed.
- 15 people wear glasses.
- 17 people have brown hair.
- 3 people with brown hair wear glasses and are left-handed.
- 25 people have brown hair or wear glasses.
- 7 people have brown hair and wear glasses.
- 20 people are left-handed or have brown hair.
- 5 people wear glasses and are left-handed.

A person is chosen at random from this group. The following are 3 possible events:

A: choosing a left-handed person
B: choosing a person who wears glasses
C: choosing a person with brown hair

a) Represent this situation using a Venn diagram.

b) Express each of the following statements using set-builder notation.

1) Choosing a person who wears glasses and is left-handed.

2) Choosing a left-handed person who wears glasses or has brown hair.

3) Choosing a person who has brown hair and wears glasses or a left-handed person who has brown hair.

c) Calculate:

1) $P(A \cup B)$

2) $P(A \cap B)$

3) $P(A \cup B \cup C)$

4) $P((A \cap B) \cap C)$

5) $P((A \cup B) \cap C)$

6) $P((B \cap C) \cup A)$

d) Calculate the probability of choosing a person:

1) who wears glasses and does not have brown hair

2) who does not wear glasses and is not left-handed

3) who is left-handed, does not wear glasses and does not have brown hair

It is estimated that between 10% and 12% of the population is left-handed. Having a left-handed parent increases the probability that a child will also be left-handed.

10 If A ∪ B = A, what does A ∩ B correspond to? Explain your answer.

11 Below is the content of three boxes:

Box Ⓐ   Box Ⓑ   Box Ⓒ

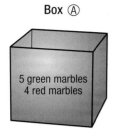 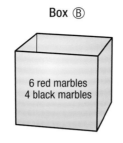 

5 green marbles   6 red marbles   4 green marbles
4 red marbles   4 black marbles   7 black marbles

A marble is drawn from Box Ⓐ and then replaced. If the marble selected is:

- red, a second selection is made from Box Ⓑ.

- green, a second selection is made from Box Ⓒ.

a) Are the compound events resulting from this experiment composed of dependent or independent events? Explain your answer.

b) What is the probability of the event:

   1) "choosing a green marble on the first section followed by a red marble" on the second selection?

   2) "choosing two marbles of the same colour"?

   3) "choosing a single black marble"?

c) In this situation, describe two events that are:

   1) mutually exclusive

   2) non-mutually exclusive

12 Using a Venn diagram, represent three non-empty sets A, B and C, such that the following is true:

a) A ∩ B ≠ ∅, B ∩ C ≠ ∅, and A ∩ C = ∅.

b) A ∪ B ∪ C = A ∪ B and B ∩ C = C.

c) A ∪ B ∪ C = C and A ∩ B = B.

13 A 6-sided die with faces numbered 1 to 6 is rolled twice. The following are 2 possible events:

A: obtaining a sum that is even
B: obtaining a sum that is greater than or equal to 7

a) Are these two events mutually exclusive? Explain your answer.

b) Calculate:

   1) $P(A)$ 2) $P(B)$ 3) $P(A ∩ B)$ 4) $P(A ∪ B)$

BLOOD TYPES The following is information regarding the compatibility of blood types during blood transfusions and on the distribution of blood types within the Canadian population.

Compatibility of blood types

Recipient \ Donor	O	A	B	AB
O	✔			
A	✔	✔		
B	✔		✔	
AB	✔	✔	✔	✔

Distribution of blood types within the Canadian population

O	A	B	AB
46%	42%	9%	3%

a) In Canada, what is the probability that a randomly selected person will be compatible with:

1) an O donor?
2) a B recipient?
3) an AB recipient?
4) an A donor?
5) an A recipient and a B recipient?
6) an AB donor or a B donor?

b) If two people are randomly selected, what is the probability that their blood types will be compatible in one way or the other?

Before the discovery of different blood types, many transfusions ended in failure because the recipient's immune system would consider the donor's blood cells, which were not compatible, as harmful organisms and destroy them.

15 Below are events related to the weather forecast for three consecutive days:

A: it will rain on Monday.
B: it will rain on Monday and Tuesday.
C: it will rain on Tuesday or Wednesday.

In addition: $P(A) = 0.45$, $P(B) = 0.3$ and $P(C) = 0.8$.

a) Calculate the probability that it will rain on:

1) Tuesday
2) Wednesday
3) Monday or Wednesday
4) Monday, Tuesday and Wednesday

b) Calculate the probability that it will rain on at least one of the three days.

Meteorologists determine the probability of thunderstorms using indices; for example, the TT (Total Totals) index is obtained by calculating the differences between temperatures measured at different altitudes.

16 A student chooses three notes randomly and without repetition from the eight notes of the C major scale shown in the adjacent illustration.

The chord composed of the three notes is defined as follows:
- It is a C major if it is composed only of notes from the set {C, E, G, high C}.
- It is a G major if it is composed of the notes E, G and B.

The following are 3 events related to this situation:

A: obtaining a C major chord
B: obtaining a chord that contains the note G
C: obtaining a G major chord

a) Translate the following events into words.

1) A ∪ B   2) A ∩ C   3) B ∩ C

b) Using events A, B and C, identify:

1) two pairs of non-mutually exclusive events

2) one pair of mutually exclusive events

c) Calculate the probability of obtaining the following chord:

1) C major

2) C major that contains the note G

3) G major or a chord that contains the note G

Some composers have introduced chance into their works. For instance, John Cage (1912-1992) composed some of his pieces using random generation.

17 The adjacent table presents the distribution of employees at a company based on sex and mother tongue.

A member of this company's staff is randomly selected for training. The following are three possible events:

A: the staff member is a man.
B: the staff member is a woman.
C: the staff member is Anglophone.

A company's employees

Mother tongue \ Sex	Man	Woman	Total
French	34	77	111
English	21	11	32
Other	10	4	14
Total	65	92	157

a) Illustrate the preceding events in a Venn diagram, and include the appropriate numbers.

b) Calculate:

1) $P(A \cup B)$ 2) $P(A \cup C)$ 3) $P(B \cup C)$ 4) $P(A \cap C)$ 5) $P(B \cap C)$

A team is randomly formed of three employees. The following are 3 possible events:

D: choosing an Anglophone staff member with the 1st selection
E: choosing a woman with the 2nd selection
F: choosing a Francophone staff member with the 3rd selection

c) Are events D, E and F dependent or independent? Explain your answer.

d) Calculate $P(D \cap E \cap F)$.

This section is related to LES 10.

 PROBLEM The two-child paradox

Below are two situations that appear to be similar:

Situation ①

Situation ②

 Why are these two probabilities different?

ACTIVITY 1 Given that...

An experiment consists of drawing, blindfolded, a marble from a box that contains:

- 5 white marbles numbered 1 to 5
- 6 black marbles numbered 6 to 11
- 5 green marbles numbered 3 to 7

The following are 2 possible events:

> A: obtaining a green marble
> B: obtaining a marble with an even number

a. In a Venn diagram similar to the one shown in the adjacent illustration, indicate each outcome in the appropriate location.

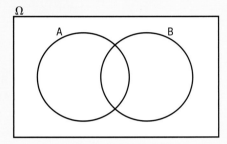

b. Explain why events A and B are non-mutually exclusive.

c. Calculate:

1) $P(A)$ 2) $P(B)$ 3) $P(A \cap B)$

d. 1) The person who drew the marble is informed that its number is even. What is the probability that the marble drawn is green? Explain your answer.

2) Compare your answer to the one that you provided in **c. 1)**. What do you notice?

e. Explain the effect of the occurrence of the event "obtaining a marble with an even number" on the probability of the occurrence of the event "obtaining a green marble."

f. Another marble is drawn. What is the probability that:

1) the marble drawn has an even number given that it is white?

2) the marble drawn has an odd number given that it is not black?

3) the marble drawn is black given that it has an even number?

CONDITIONAL PROBABILITY

A conditional probability is the probability that an event will occur given that another event has already occurred. The probability that event B will occur given that event A has already occurred is written as follows:

$$P(\text{B given A}) = P(B\,|\,A) = \frac{P(A \cap B)}{P(A)} \text{ where } P(A) \neq 0.$$

E.g. A 6-sided die with faces numbered from 1 to 6 is rolled, and the top face is observed. The following are two possible events:

A: obtaining an odd number
B: obtaining a number greater than 2

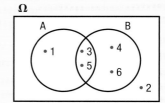

The probability of obtaining a number greater than 2 given that the top face of the die is an odd number is written:

$$P(B\,|\,A) = \frac{P(A \cap B)}{P(A)} = \frac{\frac{1}{3}}{\frac{1}{2}} = \frac{2}{3}$$

Conditional probability is involved in the calculation of the probability of an event that is composed of two intermediate dependent events A and B. This probability is written as follows:

$$P(A \cap B) = P(A) \times P(B\,|\,A)$$

E.g. Two marbles are drawn, without replacement, from a box containing 4 red marbles, 5 yellow marbles and 3 green marbles. The following are 3 possible events:

A: obtaining a yellow marble with the first draw
B: obtaining a red marble with the second draw
C: obtaining a green marble with the second draw

Therefore:

$$P(A \cap B) = P(A) \times P(B\,|\,A) = \frac{5}{12} \times \frac{4}{11} = \frac{20}{132} = \frac{5}{33}$$

$$P(A \cap C) = P(A) \times P(C\,|\,A) = \frac{5}{12} \times \frac{3}{11} = \frac{15}{132} = \frac{5}{44}$$

practice (4.2)

1 A 6-sided die with faces numbered from 1 to 6 is rolled, and the top face is observed.

What is the probability that the outcome is:

a) an even number given that it is greater than 2?

b) a multiple of 3 given that it is less than 5?

c) a factor of 6 given that it is even?

d) a prime number given that it is even?

e) a multiple of 4 given that it is greater than 4?

2 Below is some information regarding the probability of several events.

$P(A) = 0.31$ $P(B) = 0.52$ $P(A \cup B) = 0.67$

$P(C) = 0.46$ $P(A \cap C) = 0.13$ $P(B \cap C) = 0$

Calculate:

a) $P(A|B)$ b) $P(B|A)$ c) $P(A|C)$ d) $P(C|A)$ e) $P(C|B)$ f) $P(B|C)$

3 An experiment consists of drawing a card at random from a deck of 52 cards.
The following are 4 possible events:

A: obtaining a face card
B: obtaining a king
C: obtaining a red card
D: obtaining a heart

The origin of playing cards is unknown; however, it is believed that they were invented in China or the Middle East. The layout of the double head, currently used, originated in the 1830s.

Calculate:

a) $P(B|A)$ b) $P(B|C)$ c) $P(B|D)$ d) $P(C|A)$ e) $P(C|B)$ f) $P(D|C)$

4 All the outcomes listed in the adjacent Venn diagram are equiprobable.

Determine:

a) $P(A|B)$ b) $P(B|A)$

c) $P(A|C)$ d) $P(C|A)$

e) $P((A \cap B)|B)$ f) $P(B|(A \cap C))$

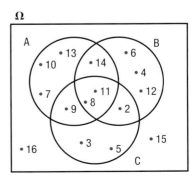

5 What can you conclude about the relationship between two events A and B with non-zero probabilities if:

a) $P(B|A) = 1$?

b) $P(B|A) = P(B)$?

c) $P(B|A) = 0$?

6 A company makes drill bits using a computerized lathe. The contingency table below provides information about the quality of the drill bits during an inspection.

Drill-bit quality control

	Not defective	Defective	Total
Number of wood drill bits	540	34	
Number of cement drill bits			
Total	1410		1500

a) If a drill bit is selected at random from those that were inspected, what is the probability of choosing:

1) a wood drill bit?

2) a defective drill bit given that it is a cement drill bit?

3) a wood drill bit given that it is defective?

If 2 defective drill bits of the same type are selected successively, all the drill bits of that type must be rejected.

b) What is the probability of rejecting:

1) all of the wood drill bits?

2) all of the cement drill bits?

7 In order to study the effectiveness of a flu vaccine, it is administered to half of a sample of 20 000 people. Of this sample, 550 people who received the vaccine and 2250 people who did not get that vaccine contracted the flu. The person is chosen at random from the sample. The following are 4 possible events:

A: the person contracted the flu.
B: the person did not contract the flu.
C: the person was vaccinated.
D: the person was not vaccinated.

According to the World Health Organization (WHO), vaccination is an essential strategy for ensuring worldwide health safety and managing the threat of emerging infections.

a) Calculate the probability of the following situations:

1) The person was vaccinated given that he or she contracted the flu.

2) The person contracted the flu given that he or she was not vaccinated.

3) The person was not vaccinated given that he or she did not contract the flu.

4) The person did not contract the flu given that he or she was not vaccinated.

b) Which statement from the preceding question do the following probabilities correspond to?

1) $P(A|D)$

2) $P(B|D)$

3) $P(C|A)$

4) $P(D|B)$

c) The effectiveness of a vaccine corresponds to the probability that a person will not contract the flu given that he or she was vaccinated. What is the effectiveness of this vaccine?

8 A nickel and a dime are tossed simultaneously.

a) What is the probability that:

   1) the nickel comes up heads given that the dime came up tails?

   2) the nickel comes up tails given that the two coins both show the same side?

   3) the two coins show different sides given that the nickel came up heads?

Although coins are usually round, they can have different shapes.

b) For each of the preceding cases, does the information provided about the outcome modify the probability of the event sought? Explain your answer.

9 **BAYES' THEOREM** Based on the definition of conditional probability, the following inequalities are obtained

$$P(B\,|\,A) = \frac{P(A \cap B)}{P(A)} \text{ and } P(A\,|\,B) = \frac{P(A \cap B)}{P(B)}.$$

Using these two equalities, Bayes' theorem can be deduced and is written:

$$P(B\,|\,A) = \frac{P(A\,|\,B) \times P(B)}{P(A)}$$

a) Explain how Bayes' theorem can be obtained from the two equalities above.

Below is the content of two boxes:

Box ①

10 black balls
10 white balls

Box ②

8 black balls
12 white balls

A person selects a box at random then draws a marble out of that box at random.

b) Without using Bayes' theorem, calculate the probability that the ball drawn:

   1) is white

   2) comes from Box ①

   3) is black

   4) comes from Box ②

   5) is white and comes from Box ①

   6) is white given that it comes from Box ①

   7) is black given that it comes from Box ②

Thomas Bayes (1702-1761)

c) Using Bayes' theorem, calculate the probability that the ball drawn comes from:

   1) Box ① given that it is white

   2) Box ② given that it is black

In mathematics, just as in social contexts, Bayes' theorem helps determine the degree of likelihood of a statement.

10 An organization uses the following two tables to establish probabilities regarding the use of seat belts use in cars.

Sample

Sex \ Age	[16, 20[	[20, 25[	[25, 40[	[40, 60[	Total
Man	150	175	200	150	675
Woman	150	150	140	250	690
Total	300	325	340	400	1365

Percentage of people who were not wearing a seat belt

Sex \ Age	[16, 20[	[20, 25[	[25, 40[	[40, 60[
Man (%)	65	43	15	16
Woman (%)	64	32	3	7

During a road block, what is the probability that the person questioned:

a) is wearing a seat belt if she is a woman?

b) is not wearing a seat belt if the person is a man who is [40, 60[years of age?

c) is a man [20, 25[years of age if he is wearing a seat belt?

d) is a woman [16, 20[years of age if she is not wearing a seat belt?

> According to many international studies, the use of seat belts reduces the risk of death in accidents by 40 to 65% for front seat passengers and 25 to 75% for back seat passengers.

11 Below are six televisions and six remote controls:

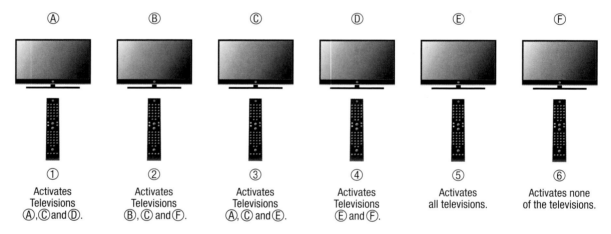

| Ⓐ | Ⓑ | Ⓒ | Ⓓ | Ⓔ | Ⓕ |

①	②	③	④	⑤	⑥
Activates Televisions Ⓐ, Ⓒ and Ⓓ.	Activates Televisions Ⓑ, Ⓒ and Ⓕ.	Activates Televisions Ⓐ, Ⓒ and Ⓔ.	Activates Televisions Ⓔ and Ⓕ.	Activates all televisions.	Activates none of the televisions.

a) A remote control is chosen at random. What is the probability that this remote control activates:

   1) Television Ⓑ?   2) Televisions Ⓒ and Ⓔ?   3) Televisions Ⓐ, Ⓑ or Ⓕ?

b) What is the probability that the selected remote control is:

   1) Remote control ③ given that it activates Television Ⓒ?

   2) Remote control ① given that it does not activate Television Ⓕ?

   3) a remote control that activates Televisions Ⓔ and Ⓕ given that it does not activate Television Ⓑ?

c) Ali chooses a remote control at random and claims that there is a 1 in 6 chance that it will turn on all the televisions. He tests the remote control and activates Television Ⓑ. Has the probability that this remote control turns on all the televisions increased or decreased? Explain your answer.

The contingency table below presents a portion of the results of two anti-doping tests performed on male cyclists following a competition.

Anti-doping tests

	Presence of EPO	Probability that a cyclist tested positive (%)	Probability that a cyclist tested negative (%)	Total (%)
Presence of growth hormones				
Probability that a cyclist tested positive (%)			9.375	
Probability that a cyclist tested negative (%)		6.25		75
Total (%)		21.875		

a) Complete the table provided above.

b) What is the probability that a randomly selected cyclist had a positive result on both tests given that he had a positive result on one of the two tests?

Even if it has the potential of causing serious health problems related to arterial hypertension, EPO, or Erythropoietin, is used by certain athletes to improve their performance because it increases red blood cells in the blood.

13 The following is some information about three collectible coins:

- 75% of collectors have at least one of the 3 coins.
- 35% of collectors have Coin **A**, 30% have Coin **B**, and 42.5% have Coin **C**.
- 27 collectors have Coins **A** and **B**, 45 have Coins **B** and **C**, and 54 have Coins **A** and **C**.
- 5% of collectors only have Coins **A** and **B**.
- In total, 90 collectors do not have any of these coins.

a) How many collectors are there?

A collector is chosen at random.

b) What is the probability that this collector has all three coins?

c) What is the probability that this collector has all three coins given that he has:
   1) Coins **A** and **C**?
   2) two coins, including Coin **A**?

The value of collectable coins depends on their age, their rarity, their condition and the metal they are made of.

14 In the adjacent figure, the sides of the two squares and the diameter of the circle are equal in length. What is the probability that a randomly chosen point on this figure is located in:

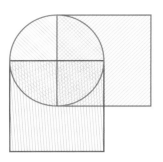

a) the red region given that the point is located in the blue region?

b) the green region given that the point is located in the red region?

c) the blue region given that the point is located in the green region?

d) the region with three colours given that the point is located in a region with at least two colours?

15 A person goes to sleep on Sunday night expecting a package. It is estimated that there is:

- a 70% probability that the person will wake up on Monday and a probability of 30% that the person will wake up on Tuesday

- a 90% probability that the package will arrive on Monday and a probability of 10% that it will arrive on Tuesday

- an 80% probability that it will rain on Monday and a probability of 40% that it will rain on Tuesday

a) Create the probability tree associated with this situation.

b) What is the probability that this person wakes up:

1) on Monday, and it is raining?

2) on Monday, and it is not raining?

3) on Monday, it is raining and the package has arrived?

4) on Tuesday, it is not raining and the package has not arrived?

c) 1) This person wakes up, opens the curtains and notices that it is raining. What is the probability that it is:

i) Monday?   ii) Tuesday?

2) In addition, the person notices that the package has not arrived. What is the probability that it is:

i) Monday?   ii) Tuesday?

PROBLEM The student council

In a school, each class must elect a student to sit on the student council. In a class of 33 students, three candidates come forward: Julie, Mahmoud and Elsa. The adjacent illusatration is of the ballot that each student in the class must fill out.

Who should represent you on the student council?
Rank the three candidates according to your preferences.

Candidates	Preferences	
Julie Mahmoud Elsa	1st choice	
	2nd choice	
	3rd choice	

The following are the results:

Number of students who ranked the candidates in this way	10	7	7	6	3
1st choice	Mahmoud	Julie	Elsa	Julie	Elsa
2nd choice	Elsa	Mahmoud	Mahmoud	Elsa	Julie
3rd choice	Julie	Elsa	Julie	Mahmoud	Mahmoud

Below is how the election supervisors interpreted the results.

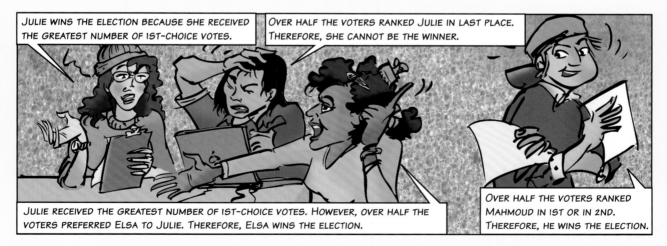

JULIE WINS THE ELECTION BECAUSE SHE RECEIVED THE GREATEST NUMBER OF 1ST-CHOICE VOTES.

OVER HALF THE VOTERS RANKED JULIE IN LAST PLACE. THEREFORE, SHE CANNOT BE THE WINNER.

JULIE RECEIVED THE GREATEST NUMBER OF 1ST-CHOICE VOTES. HOWEVER, OVER HALF THE VOTERS PREFERRED ELSA TO JULIE. THEREFORE, ELSA WINS THE ELECTION.

OVER HALF THE VOTERS RANKED MAHMOUD IN 1ST OR IN 2ND. THEREFORE, HE WINS THE ELECTION.

Who should win the election?

In a women's hockey league, a committee of 53 members must select a recipient for the trophy for the hardest-working player from a list of three candidates.

The following are the results:

Voting results

Candidate	A	B	C
Number of votes received	16	17	20

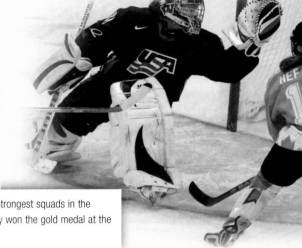

a. Who wins the trophy if the committee awards it to:

1) the candidate who received the most votes?

2) the candidate who received more than half of the votes?

> Canada's National Women's Team is one of the strongest squads in the International Ice Hockey Federation. In 2010, they won the gold medal at the winter Olympics in Vancouver.

In order to allow for a more-detailed analysis of the voting, the members of the committee are asked to rank the candidates in their order of preference. The following are the results:

Voting results

Number of members who ranked the candidates in this way	11	11	9	9	7	6
1st choice	B	C	A	C	A	B
2nd choice	C	B	B	A	C	A
3rd choice	A	A	C	B	B	C

There are several possible analyses.

Analysis ①

b. Determine how many members prefer:

1) Candidate **A** to Candidate **B**
2) Candidate **B** to Candidate **A**
3) Candidate **B** to Candidate **C**
4) Candidate **C** to Candidate **B**
5) Candidate **A** to Candidate **C**
6) Candidate **C** to Candidate **A**

c. 1) Between Candidates **A** and **B**, which do the members prefer?

2) Between Candidates **B** and **C**, which do the members prefer?

3) Between Candidates **A** and **C**, which do the members prefer?

d. Based on the answers in **c.**, who should receive the trophy?

Analysis ②

Each candidate is awarded points as follows:

- 3 points each time she is a member's 1st choice
- 2 points each time she is a member's 2nd choice
- 1 point each time she is a member's 3rd choice

e. How many points are obtained by:

1) Candidate **A**?   2) Candidate **B**?   3) Candidate **C**?

f. Based on the answers in **e.**, who should receive the trophy?

Analysis ③

g. Determine the number of 1st-choice votes for:

1) Candidate **A**   2) Candidate **B**   3) Candidate **C**

h. 1) Did a candidate receive over half the 1st-choice votes?

2) The candidate who received the fewest 1st-choice votes is eliminated. Who is this candidate?

i. For members whose 1st choice of candidate was the eliminated, the vote is transferred to their 2nd choice of candidate.

1) How many votes are transferred to each of the two other candidates?

2) Who then wins the trophy?

Another committee must select a recipient for the trophy of the most valuable player. The adjacent illustration is of the ballot sent to the committee's 74 members.

Do you agree that this player should win the trophy for the most valuable player?	YES	NO
Joyce Cramer	❏	❏
Marcelle Dubois	❏	❏
Ève Fortin	❏	❏
Patricia Lagüe	❏	❏

The counting of votes establishes the following:

- 32 members checked the boxes for Joyce Cramer and Patricia Lagüe.
- 21 members checked the boxes for Joyce Cramer, Marcelle Dubois and Ève Fortin.
- 12 members checked the boxes for Marcelle Dubois and Patricia Lagüe.
- 9 members checked the boxes for Joyce Cramer, Marcelle Dubois and Ève Fortin.

j. How many members of the committee would agree that the trophy should be awarded to:

1) Joyce Cramer?   2) Marcelle Dubois?   3) Ève Fortin?   4) Patricia Lagüe?

k. Who wins the trophy?

The medals that were distributed during the 2010 Winter Olympic Games in Vancouver were inspired by art representing the killer whale (Olympic Medals) and the raven (Paralympic Medals).

Many are called, but few are chosen

There are various procedures for electing a municipal, regional or national government. Regardless of the procedure followed, the political party that obtains the greatest number of seats leads the government.

Municipal election

- A city's municipal council has 12 seats, each one associated with one of 12 districts.
- Each voter votes for the candidate who, in his or her opinion, should represent the district.
- In each district, the candidate who receives the most votes wins the seat.

The following are the results of a municipal election in which three parties ran.

Percentage of votes received by each party's candidate in each district

District Party	1	2	3	4	5	6	7	8	9	10	11	12
A	10%	35%	23%	24%	14%	7%	35%	40%	33%	33%	31%	17%
B	43%	33%	31%	51%	11%	48%	12%	28%	31%	33%	41%	6%
C	47%	32%	46%	25%	75%	45%	53%	32%	36%	34%	28%	77%

a. Which party wins the seat in:

1) District **2**? 2) District **3**? 3) District **7**?

b. How many seats are won by:

1) Party **A**? 2) Party **B**? 3) Party **C**?

c. Which party will lead the municipal council?

- A district is a portion of the territory for which the population elects one or more representatives.
- Each elected individual holds a seat, in other words, a place in the council or the government.

Regional election

- A region's parliament is composed of 120 seats.
- Each voter votes for one party.
- Each party obtains a number of seats that is proportional to the number of votes received.

The following are the results of the last election in this region:

d. How many seats are won by:

1) Party **D**? 2) Party **E**? 3) Party **F**?

e. Which party will lead the government?

Percentage of votes received by each party

Party D	Party E	Party F
25%	20%	55%

In 2009, the Parliament of Canada, called the House of Commons, comprised 308 elected members from the 308 federal electoral districts. Federal laws are voted on in the House of Commons.

VOTING PROCEDURES

An **electoral system** consists of the set of procedures related to a vote or an election. There are several types of voting procedures. The following are a few examples:

Majority rule

The candidate who receives an absolute majority, meaning more than half the votes, is declared as the winner.

Plurality voting

The candidate who receives the most votes wins.

E.g.

Results of an election

Candidate	A	B	C
Number of votes received	23	28	12

Based on majority rule, no candidate wins.

Based on plurality voting, Candidate **B** wins.

Borda count

Every voter ranks the candidates by order of preference. If there are n candidates, n points are awarded to each voter's 1st choice, $n - 1$ points to the 2nd choice, and so on. The candidate who obtains the most points wins.

E.g.

Results of an election

Number of voters who ranked the candidates in this way	45	32	28	23
1st choice	B	C	C	A
2nd choice	C	B	A	B
3rd choice	A	A	B	C

Based on the Borda count, the number of points obtained by each candidate is as follows:

- Candidate **A**:
  $45(1) + 32(1) + 28(2) + 23(3) = 202$ points.
- Candidate **B**:
  $45(3) + 32(2) + 28(1) + 23(2) = 273$ points.
- Candidate **C**:
  $45(2) + 32(3) + 28(3) + 23(1) = 293$ points.

Candidate **C** wins.

Condorcet method

Every voter ranks the candidates by order of preference. Through analyzing the results, the candidate who defeats all the other candidates in a one-on-one confrontation wins.

Based on the Condorcet method:

- 23 voters prefer Candidate **A** to Candidate **C**, and $45 + 32 + 28 = 105$ voters prefer Candidate **C** to Candidate **A**.
- $28 + 23 = 51$ voters prefer Candidate **A** to Candidate **B**, and $45 + 32 = 77$ voters prefer Candidate **B** to Candidate **A**.
- $45 + 23 = 68$ voters prefer Candidate **B** to Candidate **C**, and $32 + 28 = 60$ voters prefer Candidate **C** to Candidate **B**.

Since Candidate **B** is preferred to Candidates **A** and **C**, Candidate **B** wins.

Elimination method

Voters rank the candidates in order of preference. The 1st-choice votes for each candidate are counted. The candidate who received the fewest 1st-choice votes is eliminated, and his or her votes are redistributed to the candidates representing the following choice. If a candidate has a majority, he or she wins the election. If not, the procedure is repeated.

E.g.

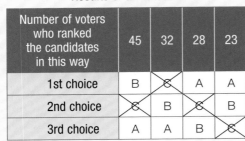

Results of an election

Number of voters who ranked the candidates in this way	45	32	28	23
1st choice	B	✗	A	A
2nd choice	✗	B	✗	B
3rd choice	A	A	B	✗

- Candidate **A** has 28 + 23 = 51 1st-choice votes, Candidate **B** has 45, and Candidate **C** has 32. Therefore, Candidate **C** is eliminated.
- Candidate **C**'s 32 1st-choice votes are transferred to Candidate **B** since he or she was the next choice for these 32 voters.
- Candidate **B** now has 45 + 32 = 77 1st-choice votes. Candidate **B** has a majority and wins.

Approval voting

Voters vote for as many candidates as they like. The candidate who receives the most votes is the winner.

E.g. **Results of an election in which A, B, C and D are candidates**

Number of voters who voted for the candidate or candidates	45	32	28	23
	A	B	A	A
	D	C	B	B
		D	C	

The number of votes received by each candidate is as follows:

- For Candidate **A**: 45 + 28 + 23 = 96 votes.
- For Candidate **B**: 32 + 28 = 60 votes.
- For Candidate **C**: 32 + 28 = 60 votes.
- For Candidate **D**: 45 + 32 = 77 votes.

Candidate **A** wins.

Proportional representation

The decision-making power is distributed among the possible choices in proportion to the number of votes received.

E.g. In a region, 10 seats must be filled.

Election results

Party	A	B	C	Total
Number of votes received	15 235	23 429	2893	41 557

The number of seats attributed to each party can be calculated as follows.

Party **A**: $\frac{15\ 235}{41\ 557} \times 10 \approx 3.67$ seats, therefore at least 3 seats.

Party **B**: $\frac{23\ 429}{41\ 557} \times 10 \approx 5.64$ seats, therefore at least 5 seats.

Party **C**: $\frac{2893}{41\ 557} \times 10 \approx 0.7$ seats.

8 seats have been attributed. The 2 other seats are attributed by placing the remainders in decreasing order.

C: 0.7 seats. Candidate **C** is attributed 1 seat.

A: 0.67 seats. Candidate **A** is attributed 1 seat.

B: 0.64 seats. Candidate **B** is not attributed any seats because the 2 remaining seats have already been attributed.

Party **A** receives 4 seats, Party **B**, 5 seats and Party **C**, 1 seat.

practice 4.3

1 For each case, determine the winner based on:

a) the Borda count

Results of the ranking of three activities

Number of people who ranked the activities in this way	17	15	12	8
1st choice	Reading	Walking	Walking	Movies
2nd choice	Walking	Reading	Movies	Reading
3rd choice	Movies	Movies	Reading	Walking

b) the Condorcet method

Results of the ranking of three sports

Number of people who ranked the sports in this way	20	14	11	9
1st choice	Soccer	Soccer	Hockey	Tennis
2nd choice	Tennis	Hockey	Tennis	Soccer
3rd choice	Hockey	Tennis	Soccer	Hockey

c) the elimination method

Results of the ranking of three desserts

Number of people who ranked the desserts in this way	17	15	12	10	8	7
1st choice	Fruit	Jello	Jello	Yogurt	Yogurt	Fruit
2nd choice	Yogurt	Fruit	Fruit	Fruit	Jello	Yogurt
3rd choice	Jello	Yogurt	Yogurt	Jello	Fruit	Jello

2 A school's administrators must choose an end-of-year field trip from among four possibilities. To do so, they conduct a student survey. The following are the results:

Results of the ranking of four field trips

Number of people who ranked the field trips in this way	27	18	18	15	12	10
1st choice	Show	Outdoor activity	Movie	Museum	Museum	Outdoor activity
2nd choice	Movie	Movie	Outdoor activity	Show	Movie	Museum
3rd choice	Museum	Show	Show	Outdoor activity	Show	Movie
4th choice	Outdoor activity	Museum	Museum	Movie	Outdoor activity	Show

Which field trip is chosen if the winner is determined by using:

a) the Condorcet method?   b) the Borda count?

3 The following diagram illustrates the roads linking four villages. The government wants to build a school in one of the villages that will serve all four villages.

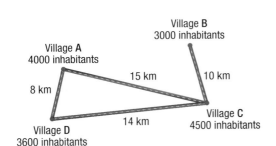

Village **B**
3000 inhabitants

Village **A**
4000 inhabitants

15 km

10 km

8 km

Village **C**
4500 inhabitants

14 km

Village **D**
3600 inhabitants

In partnership with other organizations, the United Nations Children's Fund, better known as UNICEF, made universal primary and secondary education one of the Millennium Development Goals.

a) Complete the adjacent table considering that all the inhabitants of a given village would prefer that the school be located as close as possible to their village.

b) Which village is chosen using:
   1) plurality voting?
   2) the Borda count?
   3) the Condorcet method?

Choice of school location

Number of people who ranked the villages in this way	4000			
1st choice	A			
2nd choice	D			
3rd choice	C			
4th choice	B			

c) The government plans to build a 13-km road between Villages **A** and **B** as well as a hospital serving the four villages. Given that all the inhabitants of a village would prefer that the hospital be located as close as possible to their home, determine which village will be chosen using:
   1) the majority rule   2) plurality voting   3) the Borda count

4 A group of friends wants to predict, which among four hockey teams, will perform the best. To do so, each person ranks the teams in order of preference. The following are the results:

Results of the ranking of the four teams

Number of friends who ranked the teams in this way	9	7	7	6	6
1st choice	Bruins	Penguins	Bruins	Hurricanes	Canadiens
2nd choice	Hurricanes	Canadiens	Canadiens	Canadiens	Penguins
3rd choice	Penguins	Hurricanes	Hurricanes	Penguins	Hurricanes
4th choice	Canadiens	Bruins	Penguins	Bruins	Bruins

Which team will be chosen based on:

a) the majority rule?   b) plurality voting?   c) the Borda count?

5 Elections are held in a country whose parliament contains 10 seats. This country is divided into 10 districts that each contains the same number of voters. The following are the results of the election:

Election results

District Party	1	2	3	4	5	6	7	8	9	10
A	10%	35%	23%	24%	14%	7%	35%	40%	33%	33%
B	43%	33%	31%	51%	11%	48%	12%	28%	31%	33%
C	47%	32%	46%	25%	75%	45%	53%	32%	36%	34%

a) 1) Determine the composition of this country's parliament if one seat is attributed to each district according to plurality voting.

2) Does the party in power have a majority? Explain your answer.

b) 1) Determine the composition of this country's parliament if seats are attributed according to proportional representation.

2) Does the party in power have a majority? Explain your answer.

6 In order for an organization to complete its board of directors, its 400 members must elect two people out of four candidates. The following are the results of the vote:

Voting results

Number of members who ranked the candidates in this way	120	108	98	50	24
1st choice	Angelo R.	Jeanne C.	Julie P.	Marcel G.	Julie P.
2nd choice	Julie P.	Marcel G.	Marcel G.	Angelo R.	Jeanne C.
3rd choice	Jeanne C.	Julie P.	Angelo R.	Jeanne C.	Angelo R.
4th choice	Marcel G.	Angelo R.	Jeanne C.	Julie P.	Marcel G.

The elimination method is used to determine the two new members of the board of directors. Who are they?

The European Union (EU) brings together some thirty European countries into an economic and political partnership. The Council of the European Union is made up of members from the national governments of all these countries. The number of votes to which each country is entitled within the Council is based on the size of the country's population.

7

PROVINCIAL ELECTIONS During Quebec provincial elections, the population of each of the 125 districts elects a member according to plurality voting. The table below lists the results of the 2007 and 2008 elections.

Provincial election in Québec

Party	2007 election		2008 election	
	Number of seats	Number of votes	Number of seats	Number of votes
Liberal Party	48	1 313 664	66	1 366 046
Parti québécois	36	1 125 546	51	1 141 751
Action démocratique du Québec	41	1 224 412	7	531 358
Québec solidaire	0	144 418	1	122 618
Québec Green Party	0	152 885	0	70 393
Other parties	0	9 693	0	14 167

The Parliament of Québec, also called the National Assembly, contains 125 members elected in the 125 electoral districts. The laws of Québec are voted on in the National Assembly.

a) Which party led the government in:
   1) 2007?   2) 2008?

b) Did this party have a majority in:
   1) 2007? Explain your answer.
   2) 2008? Explain your answer.

c) Describe the composition of Québec's parliament had the members been elected based on proportional representation:
   1) in 2007   2) in 2008

8

A municipality's 10 councillors are elected by proportional representation. To do so, each voter chooses 10 candidates out of 30. The table below represents a summary of the results obtained.

a) How many seats were won by:
   1) Party **A**?
   2) Party **B**?
   3) Party **C**?

The seats won by a party are attributed to the candidates who received the most votes for their party.

b) Which candidates will have seats for the following parties:
   1) Party **A**?
   2) Party **B**?
   3) Party **C**?

Election results

Party A		Party B		Party C	
Candidate	Number of votes received	Candidate	Number of votes received	Candidate	Number of votes received
1	4032	1	6356	1	345
2	1250	2	953	2	7684
3	120	3	1436	3	546
4	5504	4	543	4	2543
5	240	5	326	5	746
6	1302	6	865	6	1376
7	2074	7	2437	7	3276
8	5244	8	432	8	4527
9	1030	9	3249	9	1438
10	270	10	1321	10	645

9 **DUNCAN BLACK** Scottish economist Duncan Black applied the Borda count when the Condorcet method did not produce a winner. For each of the following cases, determine the winner using this reasoning.

a)

Election of a representative for a group of swimmers

Number of voters who ranked the candidates in this way	28	20	16	12
1st choice	C	B	D	D
2nd choice	B	C	A	B
3rd choice	A	D	C	C
4th choice	D	A	B	A

b)

Election of a representative for an organization

Number of voters who ranked the candidates in this way	23	17	10	8	2
1st choice	A	B	C	C	B
2nd choice	B	C	A	B	A
3rd choice	C	A	B	A	C

10 **ALABAMA PARADOX** In some countries, the number of parliamentary seats allotted for each district is proportional to that district's population.

The following is some information regarding four districts in a country with a 162-seat parliament.

Attribution of seats

District	Population	Minimum number of seats allotted	Remainder
A	60 000	$162 \times \frac{60\ 000}{100\ 000} = 97.2$ or 97 seats	0.2
B	30 000	▬	▬
C	9 000	▬	▬
D	1 000	▬	▬
Total	100 000		

a) Complete the table above.

b) Indicate the number of seats attributed to each of the four districts.

c) If the number of parliamentary seats were increased to 163, show that the number of seats allotted to District **D** would decrease.

In performing simulations of proportional representation in the United States, it was observed that the State of Alabama would receive 8 seats in a 299-seat parliament and 7 seats in a 300-seat parliament. This situation gave rise to the *Alabama paradox*, which demonstrates that in some cases, an increase in the number of parliamentary seats could result in a district being allotted fewer seats than it previously possessed.

This section is related to LES 11 and 12.

 PROBLEM A matter of procedure

In a country, 12 members are elected to represent the 12 electoral districts in the parliament. The seat associated with each district is attributed according to plurality voting, and the party that obtains the most seats leads the government.

The following are the results of this election:

Percentage of votes received by candidates from each party in each district

Party \ District	1	2	3	4	5	6	7	8	9	10	11	12
Ecologix	26%	33%	11%	36%	14%	13%	36%	41%	20%	30%	19%	17%
Solidarity	29%	33%	44%	37%	40%	75%	29%	28%	36%	49%	35%	52%
Alliance	45%	34%	45%	27%	46%	12%	35%	31%	44%	21%	46%	31%

The following is the distribution of voters in this country:

Percentage of voters that live in each district

District	1	2	3	4	5	6	7	8	9	10	11	12
Percentage of voters	8.4	9.1	8.2	7.9	8.6	8.5	7.8	8	8.8	9.2	7.7	7.8

The party that finished in 2nd place calls for another voting procedure to be used, namely proportional representation, claiming that if this procedure had been used to determine the election, it would have won.

> The type of voting method used can greatly influence how a government is formed. The choice of voting procedure can even be the object of a referendum.

What do you think of this statement?

A voter from the Gydan Peninsula in northern Siberia during a Russian presidential election.

ACTIVITY 1 Satisfying the greatest number of people

To determine Monday's menu at a high school cafeteria, the school's 250 students are asked to rank three menus in order of preference. The results are as follows:

SURVEY RESULTS						
NUMBER OF STUDENTS WHO RANKED THE MENUS IN THIS WAY	63	51	46	45	24	21
1st choice	A	C	B	B	C	A
2nd choice	C	A	A	C	B	B
3rd choice	B	B	C	A	A	C

a. Which menu is chosen based on:

1) plurality voting?

2) the Borda count?

3) the elimination method?

4) the Condorcet method?

When the menu selected is:

- the student's 1st choice, he or she is very satisfied.
- the student's 2nd choice, he or she is satisfied.
- the student's 3rd choice, he or she is not satisfied.

b. For each method listed in a., how many students are:

1) very satisfied?   2) satisfied?   3) not satisfied?

c. In your opinion, which of these methods leads to a result that:

1) best reflects the students' preferences? Explain your answer.

2) most poorly reflects the students' preferences? Explain your answer.

When pizza is home-made and prepared with healthy ingredients, it is a complete food that comprises the four food groups of the *Canada's Food Guide*.

The following is the description of the voting procedure used in 2 municipalities to form the 10-seat municipal council.

Municipality of Saint-Anathème

The seat for each district is attributed according to plurality voting. The following are the results:

Percentage of votes received by each party's candidate in each district

Party \ District	1	2	3	4	5	6	7	8	9	10
A	7%	35%	10%	25%	13%	35%	33%	40%	33%	21%
B	47%	12%	44%	51%	13%	34%	33%	28%	31%	32%
C	46%	53%	46%	24%	74%	31%	34%	32%	36%	47%

a. Describe the composition of Saint-Anathème's municipal council.

Municipality of Tourville

The 10 councillors are elected by proportional representation. The seats won by a party are awarded to the candidates from that party who received the most votes.

b. Describe the composition of Tourville's municipal council.

c. If the voters who didn't vote for the elected candidates hadn't exercised their right to vote, what effect would that have had on the distribution of seats in the municipal council of:
1) Saint-Anathème?
2) Tourville?

d. Of the voting procedures used in each municipality, which seems to be the most representative of all of the votes cast? Explain your answer.

Number of votes received by each party's candidates

Party A		Party B		Party C	
Candidate	Number of votes	Candidate	Number of votes	Candidate	Number of votes
1	3452	1	41 324	1	63 563
2	75 846	2	12 556	2	9533
3	5465	3	1249	3	14 365
4	25 433	4	55 439	4	5437
5	7443	5	2452	5	3266
6	13 798	6	13 547	6	8653
7	32 847	7	20 752	7	24 376
8	45 765	8	52 444	8	4328
9	15 379	9	10 547	9	32 497
10	6450	10	2850	10	13 219
Total	231 878	Total	213 160	Total	179 237

American economist, Kenneth Arrow determined five criteria that a democratic voting system should respect. He then demonstrated that when there are at least three choices and two voters, no voting system can simultaneously respect all five criteria. This phenomenon is known as *Arrow's impossibility theorem*.

The purpose of a voting procedures is to bring together the preferences of every voter and translate them into decisions for the community. Each procedure has advantages and disadvantages.

MAJORITY RULE AND PLURALITY VOTING

The following can be stated about these procedures:

- They are simple and can be implemented quickly.
- They can lead to the election of a candidate who is disliked by a large part of the electorate.

BORDA COUNT, CONDORCET METHOD, ELIMINATION METHOD AND APPROVAL VOTING

The following can be stated about these procedures:

- They allow for a more nuanced interpretation of voting results.
- They allow for the selection of a candidate who will generally lead to a high degree of satisfaction among the electorate.
- They are complicated to implement.

MAJORITY ELECTION

The following can be stated about a majority election:

- It is simple and is not costly to implement.
- It generally leads to a high degree of governmental accountability.
- It can generate many useless votes.
- It can generate a result that leaves many voters dissatisfied.
- It leads to a situation in which a party can win a majority of seats without receiving a majority of the votes, and vice versa.

PROPORTIONAL REPRESENTATION

The following can be stated about proportional representation:

- It ensures that each vote counts.
- It generates a distribution of power that fairly accurately reflects the will of the electorate.
- It often leads to a situation in which no party has a majority government. The need for coalitions among parties can then slow the decision-making process.

E.g. 1) In a region comprising 10 districts of equal population, 10 seats must be attributed, one for each district. The following are the results:

Percentage of votes received by each party in each district

Party \ District	1	2	3	4	5	6	7	8	9	10	Total
A	33%	34%	35%	40%	55%	33%	32%	38%	39%	41%	**38%**
B	32%	25%	26%	45%	40%	33%	33%	23%	32%	47%	**33.6%**
C	35%	41%	39%	15%	5%	34%	35%	39%	29%	12%	**28.4%**

If in each district, the seat is attributed based on plurality voting, then Party **A** wins 2 seats, Party **B** wins 2 seats and Party **C** wins 6 seats. Party **C** leads the government and has the majority, despite having received the fewest votes.

Based on proportional representation, Party **A** wins 38% of the seats, or 4 seats, Party **B** wins 33.6% of the seats, or 3 seats and Party **C** wins 28.4% of the seats, or 3 seats. Party **A** leads the government and is in the minority, which accurately reflects the will of the electorate.

2) The following are the results of an election:

Election results

Candidate	A	B	C
Number of voters	28	23	12

Based on plurality voting, Candidate **A** is elected even though a majority of voters did not vote for this candidate, which leads to:
- 28 satisfied voters
- 23 + 12 = 35 dissatisfied voters

These voters are asked to rank the candidates in order of preference. The following are the results:

Election results

Number of voters who ranked the candidates in this order	28	23	7	5
1st choice	A	B	C	C
2nd choice	B	C	B	A
3rd choice	C	A	A	B

Based on the Borda count, Candidate **B** is elected, which leads to:
- 23 very satisfied voters
- 28 + 7 = 35 somewhat satisfied voters
- 5 dissatisfied voters

practice 4·4

1 For each case, indicate the voting procedure that corresponds to the situation that is described.

a) In order to determine the members of the next parliament, the voters in each district vote for several candidates. Each vote affects the distribution of the seats.

b) In order to determine the members of the next parliament, the voters choose 5 candidates out of 20. In addition, the number of seats allotted to each party fairly accurately represents the number of votes received by each party.

c) The voters must choose a new president. A voting procedure should be used that allows for a nuanced interpretation of the vote and generates a winner who satisfies the greatest possible number of voters.

d) The students in a class must choose a new representative. The voting procedure used could allow for the election of a candidate who did not receive a majority of the votes.

In some parts of 19th century Europe, voting was done publicly by a show of hands. The prevailing wisdom was that each voter had to make a choice in front of the others. Today, secret ballots are generally recommended for elections.

2 The following is a statement from a country's leader:

WE ARE GOING TO REFORM OUR ELECTORAL SYSTEM. CURRENTLY, THE VOTERS IN EACH DISTRICT VOTE FOR A CANDIDATE, AND THE CANDIDATE WHO RECEIVES THE MOST VOTES WINS THAT DISTRICT'S SEAT. FOLLOWING THE REFORM, THE NUMBER OF SEATS ALLOCATED TO EACH PARTY WILL BE PROPORTIONAL TO THE NUMBER OF VOTES RECEIVED BY EACH PARTY.

a) Which voting procedure:
   1) is used currently?
   2) will be used after the reform?

b) Compare the current procedure with the proposed procedure.

3 The following is a way to calculate the degree of satisfaction of an electorate after a vote:

When the elected candidate is defined as follows, note the following:

- A voter's 1st choice, the voter is very satisfied. Each very satisfied voter is worth 3 points.

- A voter's 2nd choice, the voter is satisfied. Each satisfied voter is worth 2 points.

- A voter's 3rd choice, the voter is dissatisfied. Each dissatisfied voter is worth 1 point.

The total number of electorate points is determined and then divided by the number of voters. The result corresponds to the electorate's degree of satisfaction.

The table below presents the results of an election.

Election results

Number of voters who ranked the candidates in this way	50	30	27	24	10
1st choice	C	B	A	A	B
2nd choice	B	C	B	C	A
3rd choice	A	A	C	B	C

a) Who wins according to:

1) plurality voting?   2) the Borda count?   3) the elimination method?

b) For each voting procedure listed in **a)**, determine the number of voters who are:

1) very satisfied

2) satisfied

3) dissatisfied

c) Of the voting procedures listed in **a)**, which, in this situation, generates:

1) the highest degree of electorate satisfaction?

2) the lowest degree of electorate satisfaction?

In certain countries, elections take place in the presence of international observers because the integrity of the votes could be at risk.

4 A country's parliament is made up of one seat for each district. After an election, the winning party obtains almost all of the seats in the parliament. However, this party received the fewest votes.

a) Which voting procedure was used?

b) Explain how this situation could come about.

5 CLYDE COOMBS Around 1954, mathematician Clyde Coombs developed a variation of the elimination method that consists of eliminating the candidate who received the most last-place votes and attributing those votes to the candidates that follow. This procedure is repeated until a candidate has over half the votes. Below are the results of an election:

Election results

Number of voters who ranked the candidates in this way	84	52	34	30
1st choice	A	B	D	C
2nd choice	B	C	C	D
3rd choice	C	D	B	B
4th choice	D	A	A	A

American Clyde Coombs (1912-1988) founded the Mathematical Psychology program at the University of Michigan.

a) Determine the winner using the Coombs method.

b) Verify that the same winner would not be obtained by using the elimination method.

6 The table below presents the votes received in an election based on preferences.

Voting results

Number of voters who ranked the candidates in this way	100	60	57	48	20
1st choice	A	B	C	C	B
2rd choice	B	A	B	A	C
3rd choice	C	C	A	B	A

a) Who is the winner of this election according to:
   1) plurality voting?
   2) the Borda count?
   3) the Condorcet method?

b) Explain why it is important to determine the voting procedure before an election.

7 The following table shows the results of a survey taken before an election wherein the winning party is determined by means of the elimination method.

Survey results

Group		1	2	3	4
Group preferences	1st choice	Party A	Party C	Party B	Party B
	2nd choice	Party B	Party A	Party C	Party A
	3rd choice	Party C	Party B	Party A	Party C
Percentage of voters in this group		35	31	24	10

Following this survey, Party **A** intensified its campaign and managed to convince half the voters in Group **4**. They now have the same preferences as Group **1**.

Show that Party **A** would have been better off not intensifying its campaign.

8 INDEPENDENCE OF IRRELEVANT ALTERNATIVES The criterion of independence of irrelevant alternatives stipulates that if an election determines a winning candidate, the winner must remain the same even if one of the candidates withdraws his or her candidacy. The result of an election are as follows:

Election results

Number of voters who ranked the candidates in this way	52	41	35	33	29	21
1st choice	B	A	A	D	B	C
2nd choice	A	B	D	B	A	A
3rd choice	D	C	C	C	C	D
4th choice	C	D	B	A	D	B

a) Who is the winner of this election according to:
1) the Borda count?
2) the Condorcet method?
3) the elimination method?

b) Candidate **D** withdraws his candidacy. Who is now the winner according to:
1) the Borda count?
2) the Condorcet method?
3) the elimination method?

c) In this example, which of the voting procedures does not respect the criterion of independence of irrelevant alternatives?

9 Four candidates run in a country's presidential election. The following are the results of this election in which the winner is determined by the elimination method.

A country's presidential election

Percentage of voters who ranked the candidates in this way	30	22	21	10	9	8
1st choice	A	B	A	D	C	B
2nd choice	B	C	B	B	B	D
3rd choice	D	D	C	C	D	C
4th choice	C	A	D	A	A	A

Dubbed the "Iron Lady," Margaret Thatcher was Prime Minster of the United Kingdom from 1979 to 1990.

a) Explain how this situation could generate political tension within the electorate.

b) Explain why the election of Candidate **B** would have been a more satisfactory result for the electorate.

c) Which method would allow Candidate **B** to be elected?

> Each country has its own political system. While the United States is led by a president and Canada is led by a prime minister, some countries, like France and Russia, have both a president and a prime minister.

10 The following are the results of a municipal election that took place in a city's two districts.

Results of a municipal election

Number of voters who ordered the candidates in this way	District 1			District 2		
	4800	4200	3800	2200	1200	1100
1st choice	C	A	D	D	A	B
2nd choice	D	C	B	C	C	C
3rd choice	A	B	A	A	B	A
4th choice	B	D	C	B	D	D

In each district, the winner is determined by the elimination method.

a) Who is the winner:

1) in District **1**?   2) in District **2**?

b) Had the region not been divided into districts, would the result of the vote have been different? Explain your answer.

c) Does this phenomenon occur when the winner is determined using the Borda count?

Chronicle of the
past

Nicolas de Condorcet

His life

Nicolas de Condorcet
(1743-1794)

The marquis Nicolas de Condorcet was born in 1743 in the French village of Ribemont. He studied at the Jesuit College in Reims, then at Navarre College in Paris where, at the age of 16, his unique mathematical abilities were noticed by mathematician Jean Le Rond d'Alembert. Between 1765 and 1774, Nicolas de Condorcet published several mathematical works on the calculation of probabilities and on political arithmetic.

Prise de la Bastille, le 14 juillet 1789 by Jean-Baptiste Lallemand, 18th century, Paris, Musée Carnavalet

Aside from his work in mathematics and science, Nicolas de Condorcet embarked on a political career. In that capacity, he defended the rights of the individual for many years, especially the rights of women, Jews and Blacks. Nicolas de Condorcet played an important role in the French Revolution in 1789. Since he was against some of the ideas of the French parliament created after the Revolution, he was forced to go into hiding. He was arrested on March 27, 1794 and died in prison two days later.

His works

Between 1781 and 1784, Nicolas de Condorcet published a five-volume work on the calculation of probabilities. This work contains a section entitled "Determining the probability, that a regular arrangement is the effect of an intention to produce it." In this section, he calculates the probability that a result was obtained deliberately or randomly using the following rules.

- A regular arrangement is an arrangement that has a meaning.

- If there are n possible arrangements, only one of which is regular, and this arrangement occurs, the probability that its occurrence was intended is $\frac{n}{n+1}$.

- If there are n possible arrangements, m of which are regular, and one of these arrangements occurs, the probability that its occurrence was intended is $\frac{n}{m+n}$.

For example, on a rack on which the letters L, T, O, R, U, P and F are placed, you discover that the letters F, O, R and T appear in this order. This arrangement is regular since it has a meaning based on the rules of the English language.

Figure ①

F_4 O_1 R_1 T_1 L_1 U_1 P_3

Political arithmetic

Political arithmetic is the set of mathematics whose results are used to help leaders govern. For example, statistics can be used to determine tax rates that will be acceptable to a population.

Nicolas de Condorcet contributed to the development of this discipline through the analysis of voting procedures and the creation of his own voting method: the Condorcet method. However, he admits in his writings that his method is not perfect since it gives rise to situations in which there is no winner. This is known as the Condorcet paradox.

Jean-Charles Borda (1733-1799)

Jean-Charles Borda and Nicolas de Condorcet lived in the same era and together debated the merits and drawbacks of various voting procedures as well as their alternatives. They were both members of the Royal Academy of Sciences.

1. What is the probability that the arrangement shown in Figure ① was created intentionally if:

a) FORT is the only word made using these letters that has any meaning?

b) all words of five letters or more made from these letters have meaning?

c) all words of two letters or more made from these letters have meaning?

2. The table below displays the preferences expressed in a village's mayoral election.

Election results

Number of voters who ranked the candidates in this way	2300	1700	1000	800	200
1st choice	Gingras J.	Rouleau M.	Francoeur F.	Francoeur F.	Rouleau M.
2nd choice	Rouleau M.	Francoeur F.	Gingras J.	Rouleau M.	Gingras J.
3rd choice	Francoeur F.	Gingras J.	Rouleau M.	Gingras J.	Francoeur F.

a) Show that this situation leads to the Condorcet paradox.

b) Determine the winner using the Borda count.

In the
workplace Politicians

Their role

In a democracy, politicians are people who are elected by the population. They represent this population so that the municipal, provincial and federal laws, as well as their application in everyday life, reflect the will of the people. Politicians also ensure that the resources of the society that elected them are managed properly. In Canada, politicians can become, among other things, municipal councillors, mayors, provincial members of parliament or federal members of parliament. The politician's role varies depending on the position he or she holds.

The very first politician to hold the title of Prime Minister of Canada, following the signing of the British North America Act (BNA Act) of 1867, was John A. Macdonald. He led the country from 1867 to 1873 and from 1878 to 1891.

Members of parliament

Members debate laws, propose new ones and suggest amendments to those that already exist. These propositions are then put to a vote by all members.

The member for the Marie-Victoria district conducts a survey in which she asks her voters to rank the propositions below according to their preferences.

The maximum speed allowed in school zones will be lowered to:

Ⓐ 25 km/h   Ⓑ 20 km/h   Ⓒ 5 km/h

Results of a survey on school zone speeds

Number of voters who ranked the propositions in this way	3155	2367	1549	1435
1st choice	A	B	B	C
2nd choice	B	A	C	B
3rd choice	C	C	A	A

Senators

In Canada, senators are unelected individuals appointed by the governor general upon the recommendation of the prime minister. The senators' role is to review the bills proposed by federal members. In order to be adopted, a bill must be approved by the members and the senators.

All the senators together form the senate. This word is derived from the Latin word *senatus*, meaning "council of elders."

In December 1961, Marie-Claire Kirkland-Casgrain became the first woman to be elected to the Legislative Assembly of Québec. She was re-elected the following autumn, becoming the first woman to be appointed as a Cabinet minister in Québec.

The table below shows the results of a ministerial vote regarding a bill.

Bill: It is proposed that the maximum speed in school zones be reduced to 20 km/h.

		Members from Party **A**	Members from Party **B**	Members from Party **C**	Independent members	Total
Number of members who voted:	for	52	52	35	30	169
	against	44	27	32	31	134
Total		96	79	67	61	303
Result: the bill is adopted.						

Ministers

The term minister comes from the Latin *ministrare*, which means "to serve."

A minister is generally a member of the ruling party who has been charged with a ministry, such as Health or Education, by the prime minister. He or she is responsible for the proper management of services and the application of laws that are voted on by the members and that relate to the ministry.

Required skills

There is no specific training to become a politician. However, many politicians have a background in law, sociology or education. A political career can begin in various ways, for example, by being elected as a municipal councillor and then being recruited by a political party to run for a region's seat. People who are well-known in other areas may also be recruited by these parties and make the jump into politics.

There are many individual skills that can lead to a fruitful political career, such as an ability to create a large network of contacts, to communicate ideas, to listen and to manage a lot of information at the same time.

An unusual occurence, three members of the same family have led Québec as members of three different political parties. First, Daniel Johnson, the father, was elected as a member of the Union Nationale in 1966. Then, his two sons were elected: Pierre-Marc Johnson as a member of the Parti Québécois in 1985 and Daniel Johnson as a member of the Liberal Party in 1994.

1. The member for the Marie-Victoria district must present the proposition favoured by her voters to the rest of the members. Which proposition will be presented if it is determined by means of:

a) the Borda count?

b) the Condorcet method?

c) the elimination method?

d) plurality voting?

2. What voting procedure is used to vote on the adoption of this bill? Explain your answer.

3. If a member is chosen at random, what is the probability that he or she:

a) voted for the bill given that he or she is a member of Party **A**?

b) is a member of Party **C** given that he or she voted against the bill?

overview

1 A 6-sided die whose faces are numbered from 1 to 6 is rolled, and a coin is tossed. The following are several possible events:

> A: obtaining 6
> B: obtaining an even number
> C: obtaining a prime number
> D: obtaining heads
> E: obtaining tails

a) Are events A and D dependent or independent?

b) Why are events A and B non-mutually exclusive?

c) Represent events A, B and D using a Venn diagram.

d) Calculate:

1) $P(A \cap D)$
2) $P(A \cup D)$
3) $P(B \cap E)$
4) $P(C \cup D)$
5) $P(D|A)$
6) $P(B|C)$
7) $P((A \cap D)|B)$
8) $P((B \cap E)|(A \cup C))$

2 Following is some information regarding the probability of certain events:

$P(A) = 0.4$ $P(A \cup B) = 0.65$ $P(A \cap B) = 0.05$ $P(C) = 0.6$ $P(A \cup C) = 0.9$

Calculate:

a) $P(B)$
b) $P(A \cap C)$
c) $P(A|C)$
d) $P(C|A)$
e) $P(A|B)$
f) $P(B|A)$

3 Of the 200 students at a language school, 38% are enrolled in a Spanish course, 55% are enrolled in an English course, and 18% are enrolled in both courses.

a) Illustrate this situation using a Venn diagram.

b) What is the probability of randomly selecting a student:

1) enrolled in an English course or a Spanish course?

2) enrolled in an English course given that the student is enrolled in a Spanish course?

3) who is not enrolled in either of these courses?

French, Spanish and Portuguese, which are classified as Romance languages, are derived from popular Latin.

Uam priori anno mam, ad com talem, ecce tibi mireris, hanc, executione ultim ram initio materiam de finguli quippe quam ab aliis doctiffim

4 In a city, 70% of the inhabitants are non-smokers. Specialists estimate that there is a 45% chance that smokers will suffer from lung cancer at some point in their lives while the probability is 10% for non-smokers. If a person is chosen at random in this city, what is the probability that this person:

a) will not develop lung cancer given that this person is a non-smoker?

b) is a smoker and will develop lung cancer?

c) will not develop lung cancer given that this person is a smoker?

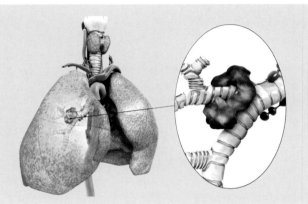

Lung cancer remains the largest cause of death by cancer, both for women and for men. While exposure to asbestos, air pollution and family history are all risk factors, smoking is the main cause of lung cancer.

5 The table below lists the most popular activities among students at a high school.

Popular activities

	Skiing	Going to a movie	Going to a hockey game	Total
Number of girls	55	34	66	155
Number of boys	87	25	105	217
Total	142	59	171	372

a) If a person is chosen at random, calculate:

1) P(girl and skiing)

2) P(boy or movies)

3) P(girl|movies)

4) P(hockey game|boy)

b) If a person is chosen at random, what is the probability:

1) that this person is a boy given that this individual likes to go to hockey games?

2) that this person likes to go to hockey games?

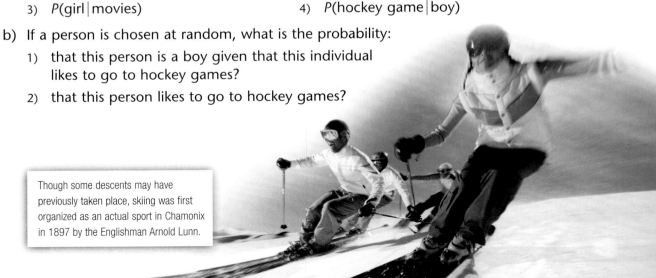

Though some descents may have previously taken place, skiing was first organized as an actual sport in Chamonix in 1897 by the Englishman Arnold Lunn.

6 On average, a basketball player makes 75% of her free throws.

a) If she shoots 4 free throws during a game, determine the probability of the following:

   1) She will make all 4 free throws.

   2) She will make the last 2 free throws given that she made the first two.

   3) She will not make the first 2 throws.

   4) She will make the first 3 throws.

b) Does making the first free throw have an effect on making the second? Explain your answer.

> In basketball, a free throw is a penalty throw that is granted to a victim of prohibited contact from an opposing player when attempting to complete a basket. A free throw grants two throws that are taken 4.6 m from the basket.

7 The 50 owners of a co-op property must decide on a new colour for the building's exterior. The following table presents a summary of the votes cast according to the owners' preferences.

Voting results

Number of owners who ranked the colours in this way	17	15	13	5
1st choice	White	Grey	Blue	White
2nd choice	Blue	Blue	Grey	Grey
3rd choice	Grey	White	White	Blue

Which colour will the exterior be painted if it is determined using:

a) the Borda count?

b) the Condorcet method?

c) the elimination method?

> Typical houses in the Plateau Mont-Royal, in Montréal.

8 In a wallet, there are 3 quarters, 4 loonies and 2 toonies. 2 coins are drawn consecutively from the wallet without replacement.

a) Create a probability tree illustrating this situation.

b) What is the probability that the total value of the coins selected is $4?

c) What is the probability of drawing a loonie on the second selection given that a loonie was picked on the first selection?

> The caribou has adorned the quarter since 1936. Prior to that, the coin featured two crossed maple branches, a design that also appeared on the dime and the 50-cent coin.

9 To elect the head of an NGO's board of directors, the members can propose the person or people whom they would accept in the position. The person whose name appears the most often is then chosen. The table below presents the results obtained.

Election results

Number of members who proposed this list of candidates	39	32	26	18	12
List of candidates	Gregory	Jean	Fatima	Charles	Marcel
	Audrey	Claude	Claude		Genevieve
	Genevieve	Genevieve			Brittany
	Anne	Marcel			

a) What voting procedure is used by this organization?

b) Who will lead the board of directors?

Amnesty International, Human Rights Watch and Action Against Hunger are all examples of NGOs (non-governmental organizations) that act on a global scale in the areas of human rights and the fight against hunger.

10 A country's parliament is divided into 10 districts and comprises 20 seats which are allocated as follows.

- 10 seats are allocated to the political parties according to the number of votes received.
- 1 seat is allocated for each district according to plurality voting.

The following are the results of this country's last election:

Number of votes received by each party in each district

Party \ District	1	2	3	4	5	6	7	8	9	10	Total
A	2500	1436	2134	2546	4365	873	3254	2456	342	3084	22 990
B	2453	2765	1434	2987	642	1664	2876	2543	1987	3879	26 230
C	3215	2322	3654	132	1007	2997	2764	2767	4007	3900	26 765

What is the composition of this parliament?

11 The following is a table of the preferences expressed during a vote:

Voting results

Number of voters who ranked the candidates in this way	74	64	50	42
1st choice	C	A	B	D
2nd choice	D	B	C	C
3rd choice	B	C	D	A
4th choice	A	D	A	B

One person is chosen at random from those who voted. What is the probability of choosing a person:

a) whose 1st choice corresponds to the winner of the election according to the plurality voting?

b) whose 1st or 2nd choice corresponds to the winner of the election according to the Borda count?

> In Québec, the Chief Electoral Officer is responsible for the conduct of elections and referendums. This person ensures that the rules of political financing are respected and guarantees that electoral laws are fully enforced. This person is the arbitrator of Québec's electoral system.

12 Ali and Janice are communicating using walkie-talkies that have a range of 500 m. Ali is at the intersection of Garnier Street and Joliette Street, and Janice places herself at a random location in the area represented by the rectangular grid below. The side of each square measures 100 m.

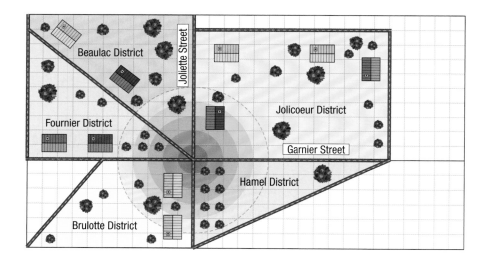

a) What is the probability that Janice is located:
   1) in the Brulotte District given that Ali and Janice cannot communicate?
   2) in the Brulotte District given that Ali and Janice can communicate?
   3) in the Beaulac District given that Ali and Janice cannot communicate and that Janice is not in the Hamel District?

b) What is the probability that Ali and Janice:
   1) can communicate given that Janice is located in the Fournier District?
   2) cannot communicate given that Janice is not located in the Jolicoeur District or in the Hamel District?

13 The following is some information about high school graduation at two local high schools in a city:

School Ⓐ students

	Number of girls	Number of boys	Total
Received a diploma	550	1250	1800
Did not receive a diploma	50	250	300
Total	600	1500	2100

School Ⓑ students

	Number of girls	Number of boys	Total
Received a diploma	630	150	780
Did not receive a diploma	450	150	600
Total	1080	300	1380

Towards the end of the 13th century and at the beginning of the 14th century, the biretta, the predecessor of the traditional graduation cap, was commonly worn by lawyers, judges and doctors.

This information is used to determine the probability that a student obtained a high school diploma.

a) What is the probability that a student in this city obtained a high school diploma:
   1) given that he is a boy?   2) given that she is a girl?

b) Between a boy and a girl in this city, who has a higher probability of obtaining a diploma?

c) What is the probability that a student in this city obtained a high school diploma given that:
   1) she is a girl from School Ⓐ?
   2) he is a boy from School Ⓐ?
   3) she is a girl from School Ⓑ?
   4) he is a boy from School Ⓑ?

d) Between a boy and a girl who studied:
   1) at School Ⓐ, who has a higher probability of obtaining a diploma?
   2) at School Ⓑ, who has a higher probability of obtaining a diploma?

e) Explain why the answers to questions **b)** and **d)** seem to contradict each other.

14 The Condorcet method can be illustrated using a directed graph in which the following is true:

- Each vertex corresponds to a candidate.
- Each edge corresponds to a preference.

For example, an edge with a value of 5 directed from A to B means that 5 voters prefer A to B.

a) Complete the graph below, which represents the results of an election.

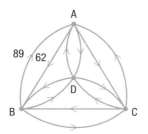

Election results

Number of voters who ranked the candidates in this way	62	45	23	21
1st choice	A	B	D	C
2nd choice	B	C	C	D
3rd choice	C	D	B	B
4th choice	D	A	A	A

Based on this graph, a duel graph can be created in which only the highest-value edges between two vertices are retained.

b) Complete the adjacent duel graph.

c) Graphically, how can the winner of this election be identified?

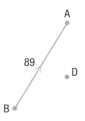

The table and graph below present a summary of the results of another election.

Election results

Number of voters who ranked the candidates in this way	15	13	10	9	6
1st choice	B	D	C	A	B
2nd choice	A	B	D	C	C
3rd choice	D	C	A	B	A
4th choice	C	A	B	D	D

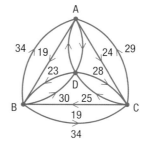

d) Using the results above, complete the adjacent duel graph in which each edge represents the number of votes by which a candidate won the duel with another candidate. For example, an edge directed from A to B of value 5 means that A won the duel over B by 5 votes.

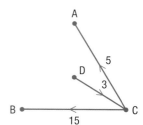

e) Explain why it is impossible to determine the winner using the Condorcet method.

f) One way to determine the winner consists of eliminating the edges of lowest value, one by one, until a candidate who does not lose any duel has been identified. Determine the winner by applying this method.

15 A district's voters must elect two representatives from among four candidates. The following are the results:

Election results

Number of voters who ranked the candidates in this way	5478	4327	3480	2530	1657
1st choice	Julie P.	Pauline F.	Antoine R.	Julie P.	Samir H.
2nd choice	Antoine R.	Antoine R.	Pauline F.	Pauline F.	Antoine R.
3rd choice	Samir H.	Samir H.	Julie P.	Antoine R.	Pauline F.
4th choice	Pauline F.	Julie P.	Samir H.	Samir H.	Julie P

Determine the winner if the following occurs:

a) The Borda count is used, and the two candidates with the most points are chosen.

b) The elimination method is used, and the two remaining candidates are chosen.

16 A country's 150-seat parliament is divided into 10 districts. The table below provides information on this topic.

Distribution of the population by district

District	1	2	3	4	5	6	7	8	9	10
Percentage of voters living in this district	14	8	10	10	12	8	6	12	12	8

The following are the results of an election that took place in this country:

Election results

Party \ District	1	2	3	4	5	6	7	8	9	10
A	10%	35%	23%	24%	14%	7%	35%	40%	33%	33%
B	43%	33%	31%	51%	11%	48%	12%	28%	31%	33%
C	47%	32%	46%	25%	75%	45%	53%	32%	36%	34%

a) Determine the percentage of votes received by each party in this country.

b) 1) Determine the composition of the parliament if proportional representation is used.

2) Will the party that wins the most seats have a majority? Explain your answer.

c) The number of seats allotted to each district is proportional to its population, and each district's seats are attributed to the parties based on proportional representation.

1) Determine the composition of the parliament.

2) Will the party that wins the most seats have a majority? Explain your answer.

bank of problems

1 A random experiment consists of rolling two 6-sided dice whose faces are numbered 1 to 6 and observing the sides facing up. The following are three possible events:

> A: the number facing up on the first die is even.
> B: the number facing up on the second die is even.
> C: the sum of the numbers facing up on the two dice is odd.

A student reasons as follows:

"Since $P(A) = P(B) = P(C) = \frac{1}{2}$, then $P(A \cap B \cap C) = \frac{1}{2} \times \frac{1}{2} \times \frac{1}{2} = \frac{1}{8}$. There is therefore a 1 in 8 chance that the two numbers will be even and their sum odd."

Explain to this student what error or errors exist in this reasoning.

2 A robot grabs an object at random from among 5 plates, 2 hoops, 20 forks, 7 full boxes, 15 empty boxes, one stapler and one paper clip. It is programmed to carry out a task based on a probability calculation. The following is some information about this situation:

Event	Task
The object taken is an empty box.	Place in the recycling bin.
The object taken is a full box.	Place on the living room table.
The object taken is a hoop.	Place in the toy chest.
The object taken is a plate.	Place in the cupboard.
The object taken is a fork.	Place in the cupboard.

Information that the programmer can send to the robot	
The object taken is a box.	The object taken is not a box.
The object taken is round.	The object taken is not round.
The object taken is a kitchen accessory.	The object taken is not a kitchen accessory.

Consider the following information about this situation:

- When the probability of an event is greater than 65%, the robot completes the task associated with this event.

- When the probabilities of several events are greater than 65%, the robot completes the task associated with the event having the highest probability.

- When the probabilities of all events are less than 65%, the robot responds, "need information."

The robot chooses a hoop and says, "Need information." Describe what information the programmer must send to the robot for it to place the hoop in the toy chest.

The notion of conditional probability is crucial in the development of artificial intelligence.

3 The following describes two situations:

> ### Situation ①
>
> Three coins are tossed simultaneously. Two coins will definitely land with the same face up. Consider the probability that all three coins will land with the same face up given that two coins will land with the same face up.

> ### Situation ②
>
> Three coins are tossed one after the other. Consider the probability that the three coins will land with the same face up given that the first two coins have landed with the same face up.

Show that the probability that the three coins land with the same face up is higher in Situation ② than in Situation ①.

4 THE MONTY HALL PROBLEM The following are the rules of a television game show in which the objective is to win a car:

- There are three doors.
- Behind one of the doors is a car, and behind each of the other two is a goat.
- The host knows which door the car is behind.
- The contestant chooses one door at random without opening it.
- Once this choice has been made, the host opens one of the two other doors behind which he knows there is a goat and offers the contestant the option of changing his choice.
- Once the contestant has made a decision, the chosen door is opened, and the contestant leaves with what is behind that door.

Should the contestant change doors when that option is offered?

The 1980s American television game show *Let's Make a Deal*, hosted by Monty Hall, was based on a well-known probability problem. This problem was therefore renamed "the Monty Hall problem."

5 In analyzing the results of a vote, the majority rule stipulates that if a candidate is preferred by over half of the voters, this candidate must be declared the winner.

Show, using three candidates, that the Condorcet method respects this rule.

6 The tables below show the results obtained after 1200 tosses of a balanced die and a loaded die.

Balanced die

Result	Frequency
1	200
2	200
3	200
4	200
5	200
6	200

Loaded die

Result	Frequency
1	50
2	250
3	100
4	50
5	150
6	600

Peter chooses a die at random and tosses it twice. What is the probability that he chose the loaded die given that he rolled 6 both times?

7 When voters deem that their preferred candidate has no chance of winning, they may proceed with a strategic vote.

Strategic voting consists of voting for a party that is liked less in order to lower the chances that a party that is liked even less will win the election.

A newspaper publishes the results of a survey prior to an election wherein the winning party will be determined by the elimination method. The following are the results:

Survey results

Group		1	2	3
Group preferences	1st choice	Party B	Party C	Party A
	2nd choice	Party C	Party A	Party D
	3rd choice	Party A	Party D	Party B
	4th choice	Party D	Party B	Party C
Percentage of voters in this group		47.6	28.6	23.8

Following this survey, the voters in Group **2** deem that their candidate will not win the election and decide to vote with the voters in Group **3**.

Submit a short article to this newspaper explaining why the elimination method encourages strategic voting in this situation.

8 In 1994, the European Parliament was composed of 567 seats divided among the following 12 countries:

Population in Europe in 1994

Country		Population	Country		Population
France		57 565 008	Belgium		10 100 631
Germany		81 538 603	Denmark		5 275 791
United Kingdom		57 654 353	Ireland		3 375 748
Spain		40 003 942	Luxembourg		402 437
Portugal		9 953 723	Greece		10 510 996
Italy		57 246 023	Netherlands		15 342 761

The table below presents the results of European elections in Ireland.

Election of Irish representatives to the European Parliament

Party A		Party B		Party C	
Candidate	Number of votes	Candidate	Number of votes	Candidate	Number of votes
1	40 322	1	9353	1	3455
2	52 344	2	23 437	2	63 843
3	14 030	3	19 436	3	5462
4	85 504	4	1321	4	25 431
5	22 460	5	41 356	5	7465
6	32 570	6	8665	6	13 767
7	27 874	7	26 526	7	32 763
8	19 602	8	51 243	8	45 274
9	29 420	9	17 249	9	14 387
10	27 302	10	9432	10	6459
Total: 351 428		Total: 208 018		Total: 218 306	

The Poulnabrone Dolmen was erected approximately 5800 years ago in County Clare, on the west coast of Ireland. It was a portal tomb and also served as a site for sacred ceremonies.

In addition, the following is assumed:

- Each country is attributed a number of seats that is proportional to its population.

- The population of Ireland elects its European representatives using proportional representation.

- The seats won by a party are awarded to the candidates from that party who received the most votes.

Which candidates represented Ireland in the European parliament?

REFERENCE
TABLE OF CONTENTS

Technology 146
   Graphing calculator 146
   Spreadsheet 148
   Dynamic geometry software 150

Knowledge 152
   Notations and symbols 152
   International system of units (SI) 155
   Geometric statements 156
   Glossary 162

Graphing calculator

Sample calculations

It is possible to perform scientific calculations and to evaluate both algebraic and logical expressions numerically.

Scientific calculations

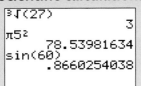

Logical expressions

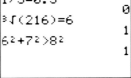

Algebraic expressions

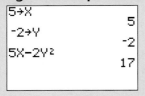

Graphing keys

Display screen

Cursor keys

Editing keys

Menu keys

Scientific calculation keys

Probability

1. Display the probability menu.

2 Display calculations and results.

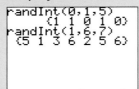

- Among other things, this menu allows the simulation of random experiments. The fifth option generates a series of random whole numbers. Syntax: `randInt` (minimum value, maximum value, number of repetitions).

- The first example simulates tossing a coin 5 times where 0 represents tails and 1 represents heads. The second example simulates seven rolls of a die with six faces.

Display a table of values

1. Define the rules.

2. Define the viewing window.

3. Display the table.

X	Y₁	Y₂
0	1	0
1	2	.5
2	4	2
3	8	4.5
4	16	8
5	32	12.5
6	64	18

X=0

- This screen allows you to enter and edit the rules for one or more functions where Y is the dependent variable and X is the independent variable.

- This screen allows you to define the viewing window for a table of values indicating the starting value of X and the step size for the variation of X.

- This screen allows you to display the table of values of the rules defined.

Display a graphical representation

1. Define the rules.

- If desired, the thickness of the curve (normal, thick or dotted) can be adjusted for each rule.

2. Define the viewing window.

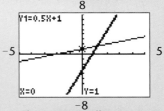

- This screen allows you to define the viewing window by limiting the Cartesian plane: Xscl and Yscl correspond to the step value on the respective axes.

3. Display the graph.

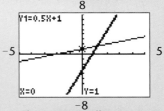

- This screen allows you to display the graphical representation of the rules previously defined. If desired, the cursor can be moved along the curves and the coordinates displayed.

Display a scatter plot and statistical calculations

1. Enter the data.

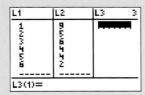

- This screen allows you to enter the data from a distribution. For a two-variable distribution, data entry is done in two columns.

2. Select the mode of representation.

- This screen allows you to choose the type of statistical diagram.

  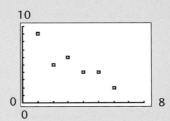 : scatter plot

  : broken-line graph

  : histogram

  : box and whisker plot

3. Display the diagram.

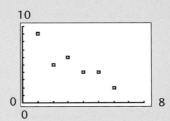

- This screen allows you to display the scatter plot.

4. Perform statistical calculations.

- This menu allows you to access different statistical calculations, in particular that of the linear regression.

5. Determine the regression and correlation.

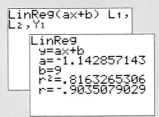

- These screens allow you to obtain the equation of the regression line and the value of the correlation coefficient.

6. Display the line.

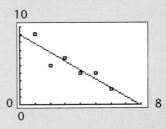

- The regression line can be displayed on the scatter plot.

Spreadsheet

A spreadsheet is software that allows you to perform calculations on numbers entered into cells. It is used mainly to perform calculations on large amounts of data, to construct tables and to draw graphs.

Spreadsheet interface

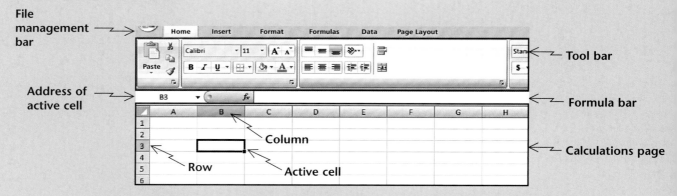

What is a cell?

A cell is the intersection of a column and a row. A column is identified by a letter and a row is identified by a number. Thus, the first cell in the upper right hand corner is identified as A1.

Entry of numbers, text and formulas in the cells

You can enter a number, text or a formula in a cell after clicking on it. Formulas allow you to perform calculations on numbers already entered in the cells. To enter a formula in a cell, just select it and begin by entering the "=" symbol.

E.g.
Column **A** contains the data to be used in the calculations.

In the spreadsheet, certain functions are predefined to calculate the sum, the minimum, the maximum, the mode, the median, the mean and the mean deviation of a set of data.

	A	B	C	
1	Results			
2	27.4	Number of data	17	=COUNT(A2:A18)
3	30.15			
4	15	Sum	527	=SUM(A2:A18)
5	33.8			
6	12.3	Minimum	12.3	=MIN(A2:A18)
7	52.6			
8	28.75	Maximum	52.6	=MAX(A2:A18)
9	38.25			
10	21.8	Mode	33.8	=MODE(A2:A18)
11	35			
12	29.5	Median	30.15	=MEDIAN(A2:A18)
13	27.55			
14	33.8	Average	31	=AVERAGE(A2:A18) or =C4/C2
15	15			
16	33.8	Mean deviation	8.417647059	=MEAN DEVIATION (A2:A18)
17	50			
18	42.3			
19				

How to construct a graph

Below is a procedure for drawing a graph using a spreadsheet.

1) Select the range of data.

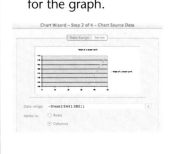

2) Select from the graph assistant.

3) Choose the graph type.

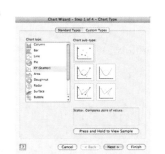

4) Confirm the data for the graph.

5) Choose graph options.

6) Choose the location of the graph.

7) Draw the graph.

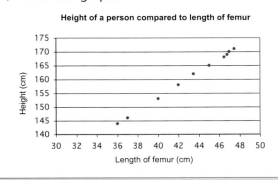

After drawing the graph, you can modify different elements by double-clicking on the element to be changed: title, scale, legend, grid, type of graph, etc.

Below are different types of graphs you can create using a spreadsheet.

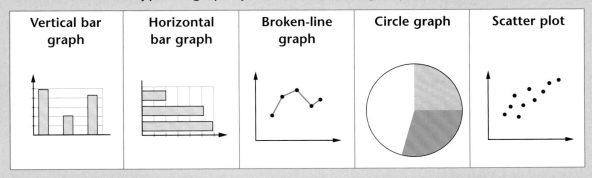

| Vertical bar graph | Horizontal bar graph | Broken-line graph | Circle graph | Scatter plot |

Dynamic geometry software

Dynamic geometry software allows you to draw and move objects in a workspace. The dynamic aspect of this type of software allows you to explore and verify geometric properties and to validate constructions.

The workspace and the tools

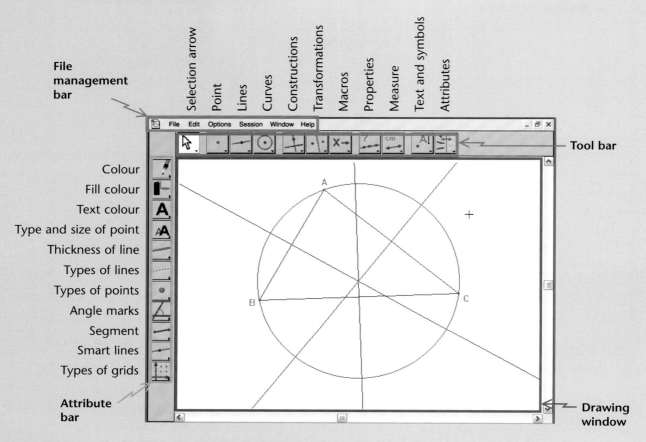

Cursors and their interpretations

+	Cursor used when moving in the drawing window.
🖐	Cursor used when drawing an object.
What object?	Cursor used when there are several objects.
✍	Cursor used when tracing an object.
✋	Cursor used to indicate movement of an object is possible.
↖	Cursor used when working in the file management bar and in the tool bar.
🖌	Cursor used when filling an object with a colour.
✐	Cursor used to change the attribute of the selected object.

Geometric explorations

1) A median separates a triangle into two other triangles. In order to explore the properties of these two triangles, perform the construction below. To verify that triangles ABD and ADC have the same area, calculate the area of each triangle. By moving the points A, B and C, notice that the areas of the two triangles are always the same.

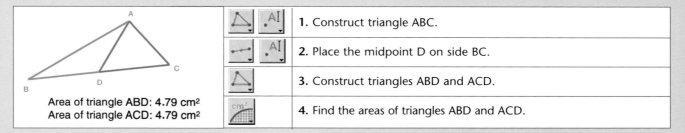

	1. Construct triangle ABC.
	2. Place the midpoint D on side BC.
	3. Construct triangles ABD and ACD.
	4. Find the areas of triangles ABD and ACD.

Area of triangle ABD: 4.79 cm²
Area of triangle ACD: 4.79 cm²

2) In order to determine the relation between the position of the midpoint of the hypotenuse in a right triangle and the three vertices of the triangle, perform the construction below. By moving points A, B, and C, note that the midpoint of the hypotenuse of a right triangle is equidistant from its three vertices.

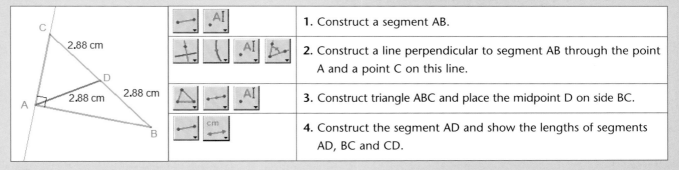

	1. Construct a segment AB.
	2. Construct a line perpendicular to segment AB through the point A and a point C on this line.
	3. Construct triangle ABC and place the midpoint D on side BC.
	4. Construct the segment AD and show the lengths of segments AD, BC and CD.

Graphical exploration

In order to discover the relation between the slopes of two perpendicular lines in the Cartesian plane, perform the construction below. By showing the product of the slopes and modifying the inclination of one of the lines, note a particular property of these slopes: the product of the slopes of these two perpendicular lines is -1.

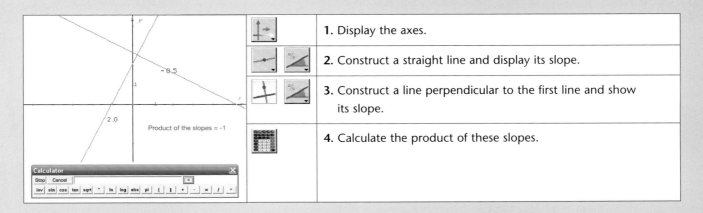

	1. Display the axes.
	2. Construct a straight line and display its slope.
	3. Construct a line perpendicular to the first line and show its slope.
	4. Calculate the product of these slopes.

Notations and symbols

Notation & symbols	Meaning
{ }	Brace brackets, used to identify the elements in a set
$\mathbb{N}$	The set of Natural numbers
$\mathbb{Z}$	The set of Integers
$\mathbb{Q}$	The set of Rational numbers
$\mathbb{Q}'$	The set of Irrational numbers
$\mathbb{R}$	The set of Real numbers
$\cup$	The union of sets
$\cap$	The intersection of sets
Ω	Read "omega," it represents the sample space in a random experiment
$\varnothing$ or { }	The empty set (or null set)
$=$	… is equal to…
$\neq$	… is not equal to… or… is different than…
$\approx$	… is approximately equal to or… is almost equal to…
$<$	… is less than…
$>$	… is greater than…
$\leq$	… is less than or equal to…
$\geq$	… is greater than or equal to…
$[a, b]$	Interval, including a and b
$[a, b[$	Interval, including a but excluding b
$]a, b]$	Interval, excluding a but including b
$]a, b[$	Interval, excluding a and b
∞	Infinity
(a, b)	The ordered pair a and b
$f(x)$	Read "f of x," the value (image) of the function f at x
f^{-1}	The inverse of function f
$f \circ g$	Read "f of g," composite of function g followed by function f
( )	Parentheses show which operation to perform first
$-a$	The opposite of a

Notation & symbol	Meaning
$\frac{1}{a}$ or a^{-1}	The reciprocal of a
a^2	The second power of a or a squared
a^3	The third power of a or a cubed
$\sqrt{a}$	The square root of a
$\sqrt[3]{a}$	The cube root of a
$|a|$	The absolute value of a
%	Percentage
$a:b$	The ratio of a to b
π	Read "pi," it is approximately equal to 3.1416
$\overline{AB}$	Segment AB
m $\overline{AB}$	Measure of segment AB
$\angle$	Angle
m $\angle$	Measure of an angle
$\overset{\frown}{AB}$	Arc AB
m $\overset{\frown}{AB}$	The measure of arc AB
//	… is parallel to…
$\perp$	… is perpendicular to…
⌐	Indicates a right angle in a plane figure
$\triangle$	Triangle
$\cong$	… is congruent to…
~	… is similar to…
$\triangleq$	… corresponds to…
$P(E)$	Probability of event E
$P(A \mid B)$	Probability that event B will occur given that event A has already occurred
A'	Read "complement," it is the complementary event to event A
Med	The median of a distribution
Q_1, Q_2, Q_3	First, second and third quartiles of a distribution
Δx	Read "delta," it is the variation or growth in x

Notation & symbol	Meaning
d(A, B)	Distance between points A and B
°	Degree
rad	Radian
sin A	Sine of angle A
cos A	Cosine of angle A
tan A	Tangent of angle A
arcsin x	Arcsin of angle x
arccos x	Arccos of angle x
arctan x	Arctan of angle x
sec A	Secant of angle A
cosec A	Cosec of angle A
cotan A	Cotan of angle A
$[a]$	Integer part of a
$\log_c a$	Logarithm of a in base c
$\log a$	Logarithm of a in base 10
$\ln a$	Logarithm of a in base e
$a!$	Factorial of a
t	Translation
r	Rotation
s	Reflection
h	Dilatation
$\vec{a}$	Vector a
$\|\vec{a}\|$	Norm of vector a
$\vec{a} \cdot \vec{b}$	Scalar product of vector a and vector b

International system of units (SI)

Base units

Measure	Unit	Symbol
length	metre	m
mass	kilogram	kg
time, duration	second	s
electric current	ampere	A
temperature	kelvin	K
amount of a substance	mole	mol
luminous intensity	candela	cd

Acceptable units for SI

Measure	Unit	Symbol
area or surface area	square metre hectare	m^2 ha
angle	degree	°
electric potential difference	volt	V
energy, work	joule watt hour	J Wh
force	newton	N
frequency	hertz	H
mass	ton	t
pressure	pascal millimetre of mercury	Pa mmTl
energy	watt	W
electrical resistance	ohm	Ω
temperature	degree Celsuis	°C
time	minute hour day	min h d
speed	metre per second kilometre per hour	m/s km/h
volume	cubic metre litre	m^3 L

Prefixes for SI

Multiplicative factor	Name	Symbol	Multiplicative factor	Name	Symbol
10^1	deca	da	10^{-1}	deci	d
10^2	hecto	h	10^{-2}	centi	c
10^3	kilo	k	10^{-3}	milli	m
10^6	mega	M	10^{-6}	micro	µ
10^9	giga	G	10^{-9}	nano	n

Geometric statements

	Statement	Example
1.	If two lines are parallel to a third line, then they are all parallel to each other.	If $l_1 \parallel l_2$ and $l_2 \parallel l_3$, then $l_1 \parallel l_3$. 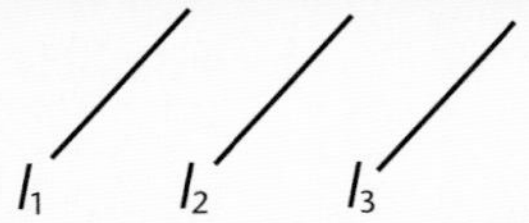
2.	If two lines are perpendicular to a third line, then the two lines are parallel to each other.	If $l_1 \perp l_3$ and $l_2 \perp l_3$, then $l_1 \parallel l_2$. 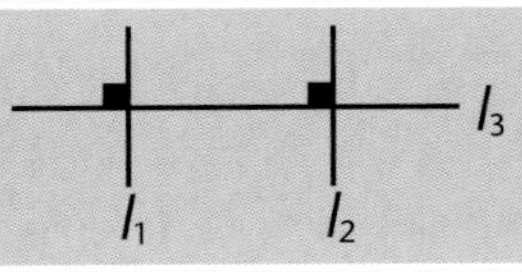
3.	If two lines are parallel, then every line perpendicular to one of these lines is perpendicular to the other.	If $l_1 \parallel l_2$ and $l_3 \perp l_2$, then $l_3 \perp l_1$. 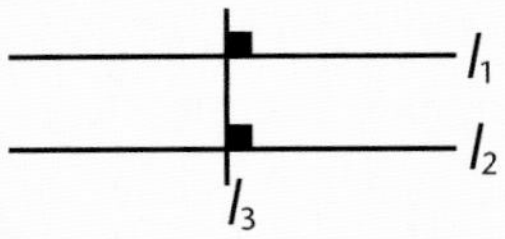
4.	If the exterior arms of two adjacent angles are collinear, then the angles are supplementary.	The points A, B and D are collinear. $\angle$ ABC & $\angle$ CBD are adjacent and supplementary. 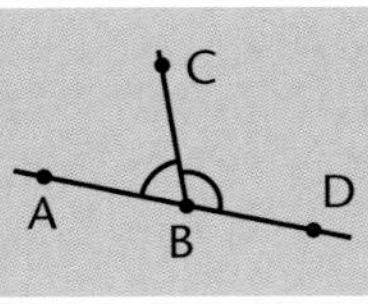
5.	If the exterior arms of two adjacent angles are perpendicular, then the angles are complementary.	$\overline{AB} \perp \overline{BD}$ $\angle$ ABC and $\angle$ CBD are adjacent and complementary. 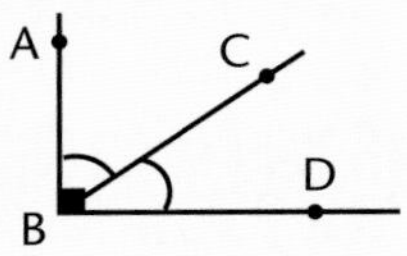
6.	Vertically opposite angles are congruent.	$\angle 1 \cong \angle 3$ $\angle 2 \cong \angle 4$ 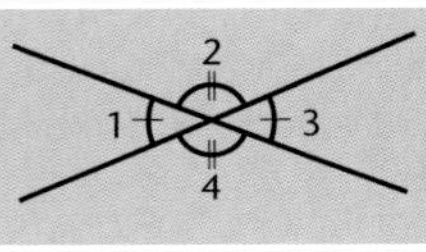
7.	If a transversal intersects two parallel lines, then the alternate interior, alternate exterior and corresponding angles are respectively congruent.	If $l_1 \parallel l_2$, then angles 1, 3, 5 and 7 are congruent as are angles 2, 4, 6 and 8. 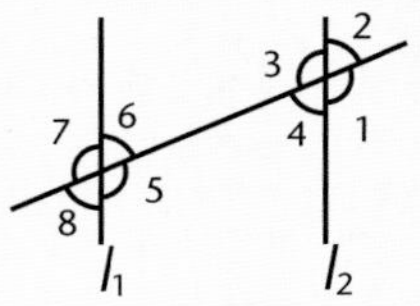
8.	If a transversal intersects two lines resulting in congruent corresponding angles (or alternate interior angles or alternate exterior angles), then those two lines are parallel.	In the figure for statement 7, if the angles 1, 3, 5 and 7 are congruent and the angles 2, 4, 6 and 8 are congruent, then $l_1 \parallel l_2$.
9.	If a transversal intersects two parallel lines, then the interior angles on the same side of the transversal are supplementary.	If $l_1 \parallel l_2$, then m $\angle 1$ + m $\angle 2$ = 180° and m $\angle 3$ + m $\angle 4$ = 180°. 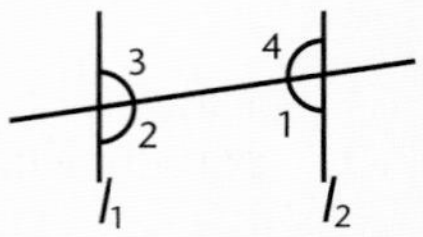

	Statement	Example
10.	The sum of the measures of the interior angles of a triangle is 180°.	$m\angle 1 + m\angle 2 + m\angle 3 = 180°$
11.	Corresponding elements of congruent plane or solid figures have the same measurements.	$\overline{AD} \cong \overline{A'D'}$, $\overline{CD} \cong \overline{C'D'}$, $\overline{BC} \cong \overline{B'C'}$, $\overline{AB} \cong \overline{A'B'}$ $\angle A \cong \angle A'$, $\angle B \cong \angle B'$, $\angle C \cong \angle C'$, $\angle D \cong \angle D'$
12.	In an isosceles triangle, the angles opposite the congruent sides are congruent.	In the isosceles triangle ABC: $\overline{AB} \cong \overline{AC}$ $\angle C \cong \angle B$
13.	The axis of symmetry of an isosceles triangle represents a median, a perpendicular bisector, an angle bisector and an altitude of the triangle.	Axis of symmetry of triangle ABC, Median from point A Perpendicular bisector of the side BC Bisector of angle A Altitude of the triangle
14.	The opposite sides of a parallelogram are congruent.	In the parallelogram ABCD: $\overline{AB} \cong \overline{CD}$ and $\overline{AD} \cong \overline{BC}$
15.	The diagonals of a parallelogram bisect each other.	In the parallelogram ABCD: $\overline{AE} \cong \overline{EC}$ and $\overline{DE} \cong \overline{EB}$
16.	The opposite angles of a parallelogram are congruent.	In the parallelogram ABCD: $\angle A \cong \angle C$ and $\angle B \cong \angle D$
17.	In a parallelogram, the sum of the measures of two consecutive angles is 180°.	In the parallelogram ABCD: $m\angle 1 + m\angle 2 = 180°$ $m\angle 2 + m\angle 3 = 180°$ $m\angle 3 + m\angle 4 = 180°$ $m\angle 4 + m\angle 1 = 180°$
18.	The diagonals of a rectangle are congruent.	In the rectangle ABCD: $\overline{AC} \cong \overline{BD}$
19.	The diagonals of a rhombus are perpendicular.	In the rhombus ABCD: $\overline{AC} \perp \overline{BD}$
20.	The measure of an exterior angle of a triangle is equal to the sum of the measures of the interior angles at the other two vertices.	$m\angle 3 = m\angle 1 + m\angle 2$

	Statement	Example
21.	In a triangle the longest side is opposite the largest angle.	In triangle ABC, the largest angle is A, therefore the longest side is BC.
22.	In a triangle, the smallest angle is opposite the smallest side.	In triangle ABC, the smallest angle is B, therefore the smallest side is AC.
23.	The sum of the measures of two sides in a triangle is larger than the measure of the third side.	$2 + 5 > 4$ $2 + 4 > 5$ $4 + 5 > 2$
24.	The sum of the measures of the interior angles of a quadrilateral is 360°.	$m \angle 1 + m \angle 2 + m \angle 3 + m \angle 4 = 360°$
25.	The sum of the measures of the interior angles of a polygon with n sides is $n \times 180° - 360°$ or $(n - 2) \times 180°$.	$n \times 180° - 360°$ or $(n - 2) \times 180°$
26.	The sum of the measures of the exterior angles (one at each vertex) of a convex polygon is 360°.	$m \angle 1 + m \angle 2 + m \angle 3 +$ $m \angle 4 + m \angle 5 + m \angle 6 = 360°$
27.	The corresponding angles of similar plane figures or of similar solids are congruent and the measures of the corresponding sides are proportional.	The triangle ABC is similar to triangle A'B'C': $\angle A \cong \angle A'$ $\angle B \cong \angle B'$ $\angle C \cong \angle C'$ $\dfrac{m \overline{A'B'}}{m \overline{AB}} = \dfrac{m \overline{B'C'}}{m \overline{BC}} = \dfrac{m \overline{A'C'}}{m \overline{AC}}$
28.	In similar plane figures, the ratio of the areas is equal to the square of the ratio of similarity.	In the above figures, $\dfrac{m \overline{A'B'}}{m \overline{AB}} = \dfrac{m \overline{B'C'}}{m \overline{BC}} = \dfrac{m \overline{A'C'}}{m \overline{AC}} = k$ ← Ratio of similarity $\dfrac{\text{area of triangle A'B'C'}}{\text{area of triangle ABC}} = k^2$
29.	Three non-collinear points define one and only one circle.	There is only one circle which contains the points A, B and C.
30.	The perpendicular bisectors of any chords in a circle intersect at the centre of the circle.	l_1 and l_2 are the perpendicular bisectors of the chords AB and CD. The point of intersection M of these perpendicular bisectors is the centre of the circle.

	Statement	Example
31.	All the diameters of a circle are congruent.	$\overline{AD}$, $\overline{BE}$ and $\overline{CF}$ are diameters of the circle with centre O. $\overline{AD} \cong \overline{BE} \cong \overline{CF}$
32.	In a circle, the length of the radius is one-half the length of the diameter.	$\overline{AB}$ is a diameter of the circle with centre O. $m\,\overline{OA} = \frac{1}{2}\,m\,\overline{AB}$
33.	In a circle, the ratio of the circumference to the diameter is a constant represented by π.	$\frac{C}{d} = \pi$
34.	In a circle, a central angle has the same degree measure as the arc contained between its sides.	In the circle with centre O, $m \angle AOB = m\,\overset{\frown}{AB}$ stated in degrees.
35.	In a circle, the ratio of the measures of two central angles is equal to the ratio of the arcs intercepted by their sides.	$\dfrac{m \angle AOB}{m \angle COD} = \dfrac{m\,\overset{\frown}{AB}}{m\,\overset{\frown}{CD}}$
36.	In a circle, the ratio of the areas of two sectors is equal to the ratio of the measures of the angles at the centre of these sectors.	$\dfrac{\text{Area of the sector AOB}}{\text{Area of the sector COD}} = \dfrac{m \angle AOB}{m \angle COD}$
37.	In a right triangle, the square of the length of the hypotenuse is equal to the sum of the squares of the lengths of the legs.	$\left(m\,\overline{AB}\right)^2 = \left(m\,\overline{AC}\right)^2 + \left(m\,\overline{BC}\right)^2$
38.	Two triangles whose corresponding sides are congruent are congruent (SSS).	$\overline{AB} \cong \overline{DE}$, $\overline{BC} \cong \overline{EF}$, $\overline{AC} \cong \overline{DF}$ Therefore $\triangle ABC \cong \triangle DEF$.
39.	Two triangles that have a congruent side contained between corresponding congruent angles are congruent (ASA).	$\angle A \cong \angle D$, $\overline{AB} \cong \overline{DE}$, $\angle B \cong \angle E$ Therefore $\triangle ABC \cong \triangle DEF$.

	Statement	Example
40.	Two triangles that have a congruent angle contained between corresponding congruent sides are congruent (SAS).	$\overline{AB} \cong \overline{DE}$, $\angle A \cong \angle D$, $\overline{AC} \cong \overline{DF}$ Therefore $\triangle ABC \cong \triangle DEF$.
41.	Two triangles that have two corresponding congruent angles are similar (AA).	$\angle A \cong \angle D$, $\angle B \cong \angle E$ Therefore $\triangle ABC \sim \triangle DEF$.
42.	Two triangles that have a congruent angle contained between corresponding sides of proportional length are similar (SAS).	$\dfrac{m\ \overline{AB}}{m\ \overline{DE}} = \dfrac{m\ \overline{AC}}{m\ \overline{DF}}$ and $\angle A \cong \angle D$. Therefore $\triangle ABC \sim \triangle DEF$.
43.	Two triangles that have three sides of proportional length are similar (SSS).	$\dfrac{m\ \overline{AB}}{m\ \overline{DE}} = \dfrac{m\ \overline{AC}}{m\ \overline{DF}} = \dfrac{m\ \overline{BC}}{m\ \overline{EF}}$ Therefore $\triangle ABC \sim \triangle DEF$.
44.	Transversals intersecting parallel lines are divided into segments of proportional lengths.	$\dfrac{m\ \overline{AB}}{m\ \overline{FE}} = \dfrac{m\ \overline{BC}}{m\ \overline{ED}}$

Statement	Example
45. In a right triangle, the length of a leg of a right triangle is the geometric mean of the length of its projection on the hypotenuse and the length of the hypotenuse.	$$\frac{m\,\overline{AD}}{m\,\overline{AB}} = \frac{m\,\overline{AB}}{m\,\overline{AC}} \text{ or } \left(m\,\overline{AB}\right)^2 = m\,\overline{AD} \times m\,\overline{AC}$$ $$\frac{m\,\overline{CD}}{m\,\overline{BC}} = \frac{m\,\overline{BC}}{m\,\overline{AC}} \text{ or } \left(m\,\overline{BC}\right)^2 = m\,\overline{CD} \times m\,\overline{AC}$$
46. In a right triangle, the length of the altitude drawn from the right angle is the geometric mean of the length of the two segments that determine the hypotenuse.	$$\frac{m\,\overline{AD}}{m\,\overline{BD}} = \frac{m\,\overline{BD}}{m\,\overline{CD}} \text{ or } \left(m\,\overline{BD}\right)^2 = m\,\overline{AD} \times m\,\overline{CD}$$
47. In a right triangle, the product of the length of the hypotenuse and its corresponding altitude is equal to the product of the length of the legs.	$$m\,\overline{AC} \times m\,\overline{BD} = m\,\overline{AB} \times m\,\overline{BC}$$
48. In a right triangle, the length of the side that is opposite to a 30° angle is equal to half the length of the hypotenuse.	$$m\,\overline{AC} = \frac{m\,\overline{AB}}{2}$$
49. The length of the sides of a triangle are proportional to the sine of the angles that are opposite to them.	$$\frac{a}{\sin A} = \frac{b}{\sin B} = \frac{c}{\sin C}$$

Glossary

A

Angle

Classification of angles according to their measure

Name	Measure	Representation
Zero	0°	
Acute	Between 0° & 90°	
Right	90°	
Obtuse	Between 90° & 180°	
Straight	180°	
Reflex	Between 180° & 360°	
Perigon	360°	

Angles
alternate exterior, p. 156 (statements 7, 8)
alternate interior, p. 156 (statements 7, 8)
complementary, p. 156 (statements 5)
corresponding, p. 156 (statements 8)
supplementary, p. 156 (statements 4, 9)
vertically opposite, p. 156 (statements 6)

Apothem of a regular polygon
Segment or length of segment from the centre of the regular polygon perpendicular to any of its sides. It is determined by the centre of the regular polygon and the midpoint of any side. E.g.

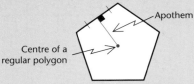

Apothem

Centre of a regular polygon

Approval voting, pp. 112, 121

Arc, p. 36

Arccosine
Operation that allows you to calculate the measure of an angle based on the value of cosine of this angle. Arccosine can also be written as cos⁻¹.

Arc of a circle
Portion of the circle defined by two points.

Arcsine
Operation that allows you to calculate the measure of an angle based on value of the sine of this angle. Arcsine can also be written as sin⁻¹.

Arctangent
Operation that allows you to calculate the measure of an angle based on value of the tangent of this angle. Arctangent can also be written as tan⁻¹.

Area
The measure of the surface of a figure. Area is expressed in square units.

Area of a circle
$A_{circle} = \pi r^2$

Area of a parallelogram
$A_{parallelogram} = b \times h$

Area of a rectangle
$A_{rectangle} = b \times h$

Area of a regular polygon
$$A_{regular\ polygon} = \frac{(\text{perimeter of polygon}) \times (\text{apothem})}{2}$$

Area of a rhombus
$A_{rhombus} = \dfrac{D \times d}{2}$

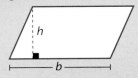

Area of a right circular cone
$A_{right\ circular\ cone} = \pi r^2 + \pi r a$

Area of a sector
$$\frac{\text{Measure of the central angle of a sector}}{360°} = \frac{\text{sector area}}{\pi r^2}$$

Area of a sphere

$A_{\text{sphere}} = 4\pi r^2$

Area of a square

$A_{\text{square}} = s \times s$
$\qquad\quad\ = s^2$

Area of a trapezoid

$A_{\text{trapezoid}} = \dfrac{(B + b) \times h}{2}$

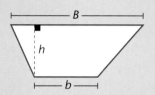

Area of a triangle

$A_{\text{triangle}} = \dfrac{b \times h}{2}$

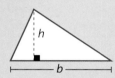

B

Borda count, pp. 111, 121, 122

C

Capacity
Volume of a fluid which a solid can contain.

Cartesian plane
A plane formed by two graduated perpendicular lines.

Centre angle
Angle formed by two radii of a circle. The vertex of the angle corresponds to the centre of the circle.

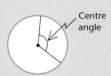

Chromatic number, p. 50

Circle
A closed line that is made of points that are located at an equal distance from the same point called the centre.

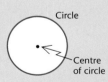

Circuit, pp. 25, 36

Circuit
  Euler, p. 26
  Hamiltonian, p. 26
  simple, p. 25

Circumference
The perimeter of a circle. In a circle whose circumference is C, the diameter is d and the radius is r: $C = \pi d$ and $C = 2\pi r$.

Condorcet method, pp. 111, 121

Coordinates of a point
Each of the two numbers used to describe the position of a point in a Cartesian plane.

Cosine of an angle
In a right triangle where A is the vertex of the acute angle:

$\cos A = \dfrac{\text{length of leg adjacent to } \angle \text{ A}}{\text{length of hypotenuse}}$

Critical path, p. 51

Cube root
The inverse of the operation which consists of cubing a number is called finding the cube root. The symbol for this operation is $\sqrt[3]{}$.

E.g.   1) $\sqrt[3]{125} = 5$
       2) $\sqrt[3]{-8} = -2$

D

Degree of a monomial
The sum of the exponents of a monomial.
E.g.   1) The degree of a monomial 9 is 0.
        2) The degree of a monomial $-7xy$ is 2.
        3) The degree of a monomial $15a^2$ is 2.

Degree of a polynomial in one variable
The largest exponent of the variable in the polynomial.
E.g.   The degree of a polynomial $7x^3 - x^2 + 4$ is 3.

Degree of a vertex, p.14

Diagram
  tree, p. 6
  Venn, p. 90

Diameter
Segment or length of segment that joins two points on a circle and passes through the centre of the circle.

Dilatation
In a Cartesian plane, a dilatation h whose centre O corresponds to the origin of the Cartesian plane and scale factor is non-zero and defined using the rule of the form
$h_{(O,\, a)}: (x, y) \mapsto (ax, ay)$.

Distance between two points
In a Cartesian plane, the distance d between points $A(x_1, y_1)$ and $B(x_2, y_2)$ is calculated using the formula $d = \sqrt{(x_2 - x_1)^2 + (y_2 - y_1)^2}$.

Distance between two vertices of a graph, p. 25

Edge
  of a graph, p. 14
  of a solid, p. 7

Electoral system, p. 111

Elimination method, pp. 112, 121

Equation
Mathematical statement of equality involving one or more variables.
E.g. $4x - 8 = 4$

Equivalent equations
Equations having the same solution.
E.g. $2x = 10$ and $3x = 15$ are equivalent equations, because the solution of each is 5.

Equivalent lines
Lines that have the same length regardless of their shape.

Equivalent plane figures
Figures that have the same area regardless of their shape.

Equivalent solids
Solids that have the same volume regardless of their shape.

Event, p. 82

Events
  dependent, p. 91
  independent, p. 91
  mutually exclusive, p. 91
  non-mutually exclusive, p. 91

Exponentiation
Operation which consists of raising a base to an exponent.
E.g.   In 5^8, the base is 5 and the exponent is 8.

Face, p. 7

Function
A relation between two variables in which each value of the independent variable is associated with at most one value of the dependent variable.

Geometric transformation
Transformation that associates an initial figure and an image.

Graph, p. 14

Graph
  complete, p. 15
  connected, p. 15
  directed, p. 36
  weighted, p. 36

Half-plane
In a Cartesian plane, the graphical representation of the solution set of a first-degree inequality in two variables.

Height of a triangle (altitude)
Segment from one vertex of a triangle perpendicular to the line containing the opposite side.

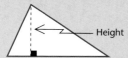

Height

Hero's formula
A formula that allows you to calculate the area of a triangle based on the length of the three sides of this triangle. In the adjacent triangle,

$A_{\text{triangle}} = \sqrt{p(p - a)(p - b)(p - c)}$ where p represents the half-perimeter of the triangle, which is calculated as $p = \dfrac{a + b + c}{2}$.

Hypotenuse
The side that is opposite the right angle in a right triangle. It is the longest side in a right triangle.

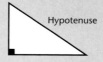

Hypotenuse

Image
In geometry, figure obtained by a geometric transformation performed on an initial figure.

Inequality
A mathematical statement which compares two numerical expressions with an inequality symbol.
E.g. 1) $4 < 4.2$
      2) $-10 \leq -5$

Inequality involving variables
A mathematical statement that contains one or more variables and an inequality symbol.
E.g. 1) $4a > 100$
      2) $a - 17 \geq 58 - b$

Initial figure
Figure on which a geometric transformation is performed.

Integer
A number belonging to the set
$\mathbb{Z} = \{...,-2, -1, 0, 1, 2, 3, ...\}$.

Intersection of two sets, p. 90

Interval
A set of all the real numbers between two given numbers called the endpoints.
E.g. The interval of real numbers from -2 included to 9 excluded is $[-2, 9[$.

Irrational number
A number which cannot be expressed as a ratio of two integers, and whose decimal representation is non-periodic and non-terminating.

Isosceles trapezoid
A trapezoid that is made up of two congruent sides.
E.g.

Laws of exponents

Law
Product of powers: $a^m \times a^n = a^{m+n}$
Quotient of powers: For $a \neq 0$ $\quad \dfrac{a^m}{a^n} = a^{m-n}$
Power of a product: $(ab)^m = a^m b^m$
Power of a power: $(a^m)^n = a^{mn}$
Power of a quotient: $b \neq 0$: $\quad \left(\dfrac{a}{b}\right)^m = \dfrac{a^m}{b^m}$

Legs (or arms) of the right triangle
The sides that form the right angle in a right triangle.

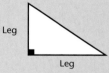

Length of a path, p. 25

Logical connector, p. 90

Loop, p. 14

Majority election, p. 121

Majority rule, pp. 111, 121

Median of a triangle
Segment determined by a vertex and the midpoint of the opposite side.
E.g. The segment AE, BF and CD are medians of triangle ABC.

Metric relations, p. 161 (statements 45, 46, 47)

Monomial
Algebraic expression formed of a single term.
E.g. 9, $-5x^2$ and $4xy$ are monomials.

Natural number
Any number belonging to the set
$\mathbb{N} = \{0, 1, 2, 3, ...\}$.

Network, p. 6

Optimizing function
Function whose rule is written in the form
$z = ax + by + c$, that allows you to compare
ordered pairs (x, y) to determine which of
these ordered pairs generate the most
advantageous solution while considering the
objective function.

Order of a graph, p. 14

Origin of a Cartesian plane
The point of intersection of the two axes in a
Cartesian plane. The coordinates of the origin
are (0, 0).

Parallelogram
A quadrilateral that is made up of two pairs of
parallel opposite sides.
E.g. $\overline{AB}$ // $\overline{DC}$
$\overline{AD}$ // $\overline{BC}$

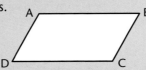

Path, pp. 25, 36

Path
Euler, p. 26
Hamiltonian, p. 26
of minimum value, p. 49
simple, p. 25

Perimeter
The length of the boundary of a closed figure.
It is expressed in units of length.

Perpendicular bisector
A perpendicular line passing through the
midpoint of a segment. It is also an axis of
symmetry for the segment.
E.g.

Polygon, p. 7

Polygon of constraints
Graphical representation of the solution set of
a system of first-degree equations in two
variables that translates a set of constraints.
The polygon is bound when the figure
associated with it is closed. Otherwise, the
polygon is unbound.

Polyhedron, p. 7

Polynomial
An algebraic expression containing one
or more terms.
E.g. $x^3 + 4x^2 - 18$

Prism
A polyhedron with two congruent parallel
faces called "bases." The parallelograms
defined by the corresponding sides of these
bases are called the "lateral faces."
E.g. Triangular-based prism

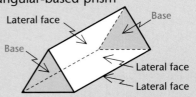

Probability
conditional, p. 100
of an event, p. 82

Probability tree, p. 83

Proportion
Equality between two ratios or two rates.
E.g. 1) $3:11 = 12:44$
2) $\dfrac{7}{5} = \dfrac{14}{10}$

Proportional representation, pp. 112, 121, 122

Pyramid
A polyhedron with one
polygonal base, whose
lateral faces are triangles
and have a common vertex
called the "apex."
E.g. Octagonal-based
pyramid.

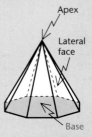

Pythagorean theorem, p. 159 (statement 37)

Quadrant

Each of the four regions determined by the axes of a Cartesian plane. The quadrants are numbered 1 to 4.

R

Radius

A radius is a segment (or length of a segment) which is determined by the centre of a circle and any point on the circle.

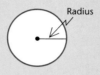

Random experiment, pp. 82, 83

Rate

A way of comparing two quantities or two sizes expressed in different units and which requires division.

Ratio

A way of comparing two quantities or two sizes expressed in the same units and which requires division.

Rational number

A number in the form $\frac{a}{b}$, where a and b are whole numbers and b is not equal to zero. Its decimal representation can be terminating or non-terminating and periodic.

Ratio of similarity

Ratio of corresponding segments resulting from a dilatation.

Real number

A number belonging to the union of the set of rational numbers and the set of irrational numbers.

Rectangle

A quadrilateral that is made up of four right angles and two pairs of congruent opposite sides.
E.g.

Reflection

In a Cartesian plane, a reflection s in relation to:

- the x-axis is defined using a rule in the form: $s_x : (x, y) \mapsto (x, -y)$

- the y-axis is defined using a rule in the form: $s_y : (x, y) \mapsto (-x, y)$

Regular polygon

A polygon where all sides are congruent and all angles are congruent.

Regular prism

A prism whose bases are regular polygons.
E.g. A regular heptagonal-based prism.

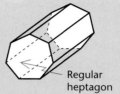

Regular heptagon

Regular pyramid

A pyramid whose base is a regular polygon.
E.g. A regular hexagonal-based pyramid.

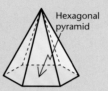

Hexagonal pyramid

Relation

A relationship between two variables.

Rhombus

A parallelogram that is made up of congruent sides.
E.g.

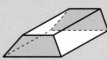

Right circular cone

Solid made of two faces, a circle or a sector. The circle is the base and the sector forms the lateral face.

Right circular cylinder

Solid made of three faces, two congruent circles and a rectangle. The circles form the bases and the rectangle forms the lateral face.

Right prism

A prism whose lateral faces are rectangles.
E.g. A right trapezoidal-based prism.

Right pyramid
A pyramid such that the segment from the apex, perpendicular to the base, intersects it at the centre of the polygonal base. E.g. A right rectangular pyramid.

Right trapezoid
A trapezoid that has two right angles. E.g.

Rotation
In a Cartesian plane, a rotation r about the origin:

- of -90° or of 270° is defined using a rule in the form: $r_{(O, -90°)}$ or $r_{(O, 270°)}$:
  $(x, y) \mapsto (y, -x)$

- of 90° or of -270° is defined using a rule in the form: $r_{(O, 90°)}$ or $r_{(O, -270°)}$:
  $(x, y) \mapsto (-y, x)$

- of -180° or of 180° is defined using a rule in the form: $r_{(O, -180°)}$ or $r_{(O, 180°)}$:
  $(x, y) \mapsto (-x, -y)$

Rule
Equation that translates a regular relationship between variables.

Rules for transforming equations
Rules that result in obtaining equivalent equations. An equation can be solved by respecting the following rules:

- Adding or subtracting the same number on both sides of the equation.
- Multiplying or dividing both sides of the equation by a number other than 0.

Rules for transforming inequalities
Rules that result in obtaining equivalent inequalities. An inequality can be solved by respecting the following rules

- Adding or subtracting the same number on both sides of the inequality conserves the direction of the inequality.
- Multiplying or dividing both sides of the inequality by a positive number conserves the direction of the inequality.
- Multiplying or dividing both sides of the inequality by a negative number switches the direction of the inequality.

S

Sample space, p. 82

Scientific notation
A notation which facilitates the reading and writing of numbers which are very large or very small.

E.g. 1) $56\ 000\ 000 = 5.6 \times 10^7$
      2) $0.000\ 000\ 008 = 8 \times 10^{-9}$

Section of a solid
The face obtained when a plane cuts a solid. E.g.

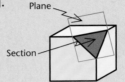

The section obtained by the intersection of this plane with this cube is a triangle.

Sector
Portion of a circle defined by two radii.

Similar figures
Two figures are similar if and only if enlargement or reduction of one results in a figure congruent to the other.

Simple event, p. 82

Sine law, p. 161 (statement 49)

Sine of an angle
In a right triangle where A is the vertex of the acute angle:

$$\sin A = \frac{\text{length of leg opposite to } \angle A}{\text{length of hypotenuse}}$$

Slant height of a regular pyramid

Segment from the apex perpendicular to any side of the polygon forming the base of the pyramid. It corresponds to the altitude of a triangle which forms a lateral face.
E.g.

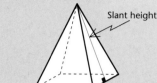
Slant height

Slant height of a right circular cone

Segment or length of a segment defined by the apex and any point on edge of the base.
E.g.

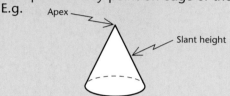
Apex
Slant height

Slope

A number that describes the inclination of a segment or a line. In a Cartesian plane, the slope **a** of a segment or a line passing through the points $A(x_1, y_1)$ and $B(x_2, y_2)$ is calculated using the formula $a = \dfrac{y_2 - y_1}{x_2 - x_1}$.

Solid, p. 7

Sphere

The set of all points in space at a given distance (radius) from a given point (centre).

Centre   Sphere

Square

A quadrilateral that is made up of four congruent sides and four congruent angles.
E.g.

Square root

The inverse of the operation which consists of squaring a positive number is called finding the square root. The symbol for this operation is $\sqrt{}$.
E.g. The square root of 25, written $\sqrt{25}$, is 5.
   Note: $\sqrt{25}$ is called a "radical" and 25 is called the "radicand."

System of equations

A set of at least two equations.

System of inequalities

A set of at least two inequalities.

T

Tangent of an angle

In a right triangle where A is the vertex of the acute angle:

$$\tan A = \frac{\text{length of leg opposite to } \angle A}{\text{length of leg adjacent to } \angle A}$$

Terms

Algebraic term

A term can be composed of one number or of a product of numbers and variables.
E.g. 9, x and $3xy^2$ are terms.

Coefficient of a term

The number preceding the variable(s) of an algebraic term.
E.g. In the algebraic expression $x + 6xy - 4.7y$, 1, 6 and 4.7 are, respectively, the coefficients of the first, second and third terms.

Like terms

Terms composed of constant terms or the same variables raised to the same exponents.
E.g. 1) $8ax^2$ and ax^2 are like terms.
      2) 8 and 17 are like terms.

Translation

In a Cartesian plane, a translation t of a units parallel to the x-axis, and b units parallel to the y-axis is defined using a rule of the form $t_{(a, b)}: (x, y) \mapsto (x + a, y + b)$.

Trapezoid

A quadrilateral that is made up of a pair of parallel sides.
E.g. AB // CD

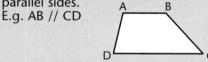
A   B
D   C

Tree, p. 36

Tree of minimum or maximum values, p. 49

Triangle
A polygon that has three sides.

Classification of triangles

Characteristics	Name	Representation
No congruent sides	Scalene	
Two congruent sides	Isosceles	
All sides congruent	Equilateral	
Three acute angles	Acute triangle	
One obtuse angle	Obtuse triangle	
One right angle	Right triangle	
Two congruent angles	Isoangular triangle	
All angles congruent	Equiangular triangle	

Trigonometric formula
A formula that allows you to calculate the area of a triangle based on the length of two sides of this triangle and the angle contained between these two angles. In the triangle below,

$$A_{triangle} = \frac{a \times b \times \sin C}{2}$$

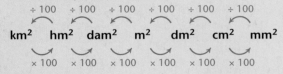

U

Union of two sets, p. 90

Units of area
The square metre is the basic unit of area in the metric system (SI).

$$\div 100 \quad \div 100 \quad \div 100 \quad \div 100 \quad \div 100 \quad \div 100$$

$$km^2 \quad hm^2 \quad dam^2 \quad m^2 \quad dm^2 \quad cm^2 \quad mm^2$$

$$\times 100 \quad \times 100 \quad \times 100 \quad \times 100 \quad \times 100 \quad \times 100$$

Units of capacity
The litre is the basic unit of capacity in the metric system (SI).

Units of length
The metre is the basic unit of length in the metric system (SI).

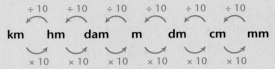

Units of volume
The cubic metre is the basic unit of volume in the metric system (SI).

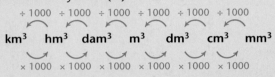

V

Variable
A symbol (generally a letter) which can take different values.

Vertex
of a graph, p. 14
of a polygon, p. 7
of a solid, p. 7

Volume
A measure of the space occupied by a solid, volume is expressed in cubic units.

Volume of a right circular cone
$$V_{cone} = \frac{(\text{area of base}) \times (\text{height})}{3}$$

Volume of a right circular cylinder
$$V_{\text{right-circular cylinder}} = (\text{area of base}) \times (\text{height})$$

Volume of a right prism
$$V_{\text{right prism}} = (\text{area of base}) \times (\text{height})$$

Volume of a right pyramid
$$V_{pyramid} = \frac{(\text{area of base}) \times (\text{height})}{3}$$

Volume of a sphere

$$V_{sphere} = \frac{4\pi r^3}{3}$$

Voting procedures, pp. 111, 112

Weight
  of a circuit, p. 36
  of a path, p. 36

Weighted mean, p. 90

x-axis (horizontal)
A scaled line which allows you to determine the *x*-value (abscissa) of any point in the Cartesian plane.

x-intercept (zero)
In a Cartesian plane, an *x*-intercept is the *x*-value (abscissa) of an intersection point of a curve with the *x*-axis.

x-value (abscissa)
The first coordinate of a point in the Cartesian plane.
E.g. The *x*-value (abscissa) of the point (5, -2) is 5.

y-axis (vertical)
A scaled line which allows you to determine the *y*-value (ordinate) of any point in the Cartesian plane.

y-intercept (initial value)
In a Cartesian plane, the *y*-intercept is the *y*-value (ordinate) of an intersection point of a curve with the *y*-axis

y-value (ordinate)
The second coordinate of a point in the Cartesian plane.
E.g. The *y*-value (ordinate) of the point (5, -2) is -2.

Photography Credits

T Top B Bottom L Left R Right C Center BG Background

Cover

(1) © Comstock Select/Corbis

Vision 3

3 TR © Gerard Lodriguss/Photo Researchers/Publiphoto 3 ML © Seth Resnick/Science Faction/Corbis 3 TL © David Jay Zimmerman/Corbis 3 MR © Dreamstime 5 BR *Portrait of the Mathematician Leonhard Euler*, oil on canvas, anonymous artist/State Central Artillery Museum, St. Petersburg/The Bridgeman Art Library 8 MR © Robert Holmes/CORBIS 9 B © iStockphoto 11 TR © Biosphoto/Sylvain Cordier/Peter Arnold Inc. 12 MR © STM archives 13 B © Acitore/Dreamstime 17 BR © Dreamstime 21 MR © David Nagy/ Shutterstock 21 B © BESTWEB/Shutterstock 22 TR © Detlev van Ravenswaay/SPL/Publiphoto 22 BR © T. Dudok de Wit 23 BR © Pichugin Dmitry/Shutterstock 24 B © iStockphoto 29 MR Public domain 31 TL © iStockphoto 32 BR © Maridav/Shutterstock 33 B © iStockphoto 34 B © iStockphoto 35 MR © Cpimages 35 B © Tyler Olson/Shutterstock 38 BR © Radius Images/Corbis 40 MR © Chris Jenner/Shutterstock 41 B © Howard Sandler/Shutterstock 42 B © Galyna Andrushko/Shutterstock 43 MR © Albert Barr/Shutterstock 46 TR The Bridgeman Art Library/Getty Images 46 MR Hulton Archive/Getty Images 47 H © 2008 Strait Crossing Bridge Limited 53 TR © dgbomb/Shutterstock 54 MR © Rob Wilson/Shutterstock 55 M © iStockphoto 56 BR © dbimages/Alamy 58 B © kmiragaya/Shutterstock 60 TL © Gena Hahn 61 TR © Koshevnyk/Shutterstock 62 TR © iStockphoto 63 TR © Hans Neleman/Corbis 63 BR © yuyangc/Shutterstock 64 MR © Blaz Kure/Shutterstock 66 MR © Radhoose/Shutterstock 67 B © Bettmann/Corbis 71 M © ZUMA Press/KEYSTONE Press 72 B © Jacques Langevin/Sygma/Corbis 73 TR © Corbis 76 ML © iStockphoto 76 BR © Maïenga

Vision 4

79 TL © Andrew Paterson/Alamy 79 TR © iStockphoto 79 ML © iStockphoto 79 MR © Megapress 81 BR © iStockphoto 84 M © Duane Raver/Corbis 85 BR Courtesy of the Société de l'assurance automobile du Québec 86 TR © Maksim Shmeljov/Shutterstock 87 MR Courtesy of History of Medicine/The National Library of Medicine 89 BR © stoyanvassev/Shutterstock 92 MR © pavelr/Shutterstock 92 BL © vikiri/Shutterstock 92 BR © Neil Farrin/JAI/Corbis 93 MR © iStockphoto 94 BL © iStockphoto 96 ML © iStockphoto 96 B © fotofriends/Shutterstock 97 TR © Régis Bossu/Sygma/Corbis 101 M © Shutterstock 102 TR © HomeStudio/Shutterstock 102 MR © Alexander Raths/Shutterstock 103 TR © Jeff Daly/Visuals Unlimited/Corbis 103 BR Public domain 105 MR © iStockphoto 105 BR © Hoberman Collection/Corbis 108 TR © Fred Greenslade/Reuters/Corbis 109 BR © VANOC/COVAN 110 BR © Rob Zabrowski/ Shutterstock 114 TR © Marc Simon/Sygma/Corbis 115 BR © Sergey Shustov/Shutterstock 116 MR © Maridav/Shutterstock 118 B © B&C Alexander/Shutterstock 119 B © Inga Nielsen/Shutterstock 123 TR *"Our Motion is Carried!"*, 19th century, work of Antal Gorosy/Private Collection/Archives Charmet/The Bridgeman Art Library 124 BR © AFP/Getty Images 127 TR © David Cole/Alamy 128 TL © mediacolor's/Alamy 128 MR Scala/Art Resource, NY 128 MR Courtesy of l'Institut national d'études démographiques, Paris 129 ML © North Wind Picture Archives/Alamy 130 TL Bibliothèque et Archives Canada/C-006513 130 BR © Tom McNemar/Shutterstock 131 TR E10,S44,SS1,D70-163,P11/Fonds Ministère des Communications/Claire Kirkland Casgrain, ministre du Tourisme/Jules Rochon, July 1970/Centres d'archives du Québec 132 BR © JCVStock/Shutterstock 133 TL © 3D4Medical.com/Shutterstock 133 BR © Mike Powell/Corbis 134 TR © Image Source/Corbis 134 MR © Megapress 134 BR © Jupiterimages/Ablestock/Alamy 135 ML © Paul Pickard/Alamy 136 TR © Directeur général des élections du Québec/photographe, John Redmond 137 TR © blueking/Shutterstock 140 BR © Victor de Schwanberg/SPL/Publiphoto 141 B © ABC via Getty Images 143 MR © Destinations/Corbis